AF589107

Janice Cosby Adams

Gray-Fully

Wisdom From My Hair

A Memoir

Honey Tree Publishing
www.honeytreepublishingus.com

ISBN: 979-8-234-03669-8
First Edition

Gray-Fully: Wisdom From My Hair (A Memoir)

 This book is a work of original authorship. Generative Artificial Intelligence tools assisted in developing the cover design for this publication.

For permissions, inquiries, or more information, please contact:
Janice Cosby Adams at www.jansgrayglam.com or
janice.cosby@yahoo.com

Adams Cosby, Janice, 1956- *Gray-Fully: Wisdom From My Hair* (A Memoir)

1. Motivational. 2. Hair. 3. Trade.

Edited by Dr. Tytianna Ringstaff

Cover Photo: George McKenney, Georgeous Images
Printed in the United States of America

DEDICATION

This book is dedicated to all of the beautiful women in my life. The women who have raised me, nurtured me, protected me, assisted me, challenged me, comforted me, checked me, and lifted me.

I am eternally grateful to my birth mother, Clora Elizabeth Cosby, who left this world way too early, and to my God-given mother, Connie Bussey Cosby. Thank you, CC, for your many sacrifices and love.

To my love and husband, Dean Adams, for always lovingly supporting me, and to the best sons any woman could have— Brandon and Zachary Cunningham— you are my heartbeat and my biggest supporters. Your unconditional love carries me. To my daughter-in-love, Jessica Cunningham, and to my brilliant, adorable grandsons, Harper, Brandon, Jr., and Kobe— I love you more than you could ever know.

To my sisters, Natalie Cosby and Sylvia Cosby Jones— I love you and can't imagine being in this world without you. You both bring me joy.

To my brothers— Kevin Cosby— my first best friend and my rock. Matthew Cosby— You are amazing, and I'm so proud of the man you've become. Laken Cosby, III (Tres)— thank you for being your authentic, loving self; and to Jonathan Cosby— thank you for your commitment to our family and loving your big sis unconditionally. To my aunt and uncle, Drs. Monroe and Jill Bussey Harris, your support and love over the years have been tremendous— thank you!

And finally a huge THANK YOU and shout out to the beautiful, precious women who have had a huge impact on my life: Carla Jones, Kristi Plain, Terri Moon, Anne Watson, Beverly Hibbler, Barbara Bridges, Sharyl Smith, Veronica Murff, Bonnie Cosby, Christine Cosby Gaither, Nicole Tate, Chevelle Roman, Gwen Rhodes, Barbara Whittaker, Juliette Okotie-Eboh, Denise Brooks Williams, Mearon Lewers, Zakiyyah Raymore, Timothie Tinsley-Glenn, Rosie Reebel, Jessica Byrd, Stesha Mays, Lyudviga Shneyders, Leslie Griffin, all of the women of The Girl Friends, Inc., and to Principal Sonia Jackson, and all staff and teachers at Levey Middle School in Southfield, Michigan.

This book is also dedicated to the memories of my older sister, Pamela Dean Cosby; Joyce Watkins; Dr. Patricia A. Maryland; Jacqueline Martin; and Janice Simmons. May you rest in heaven.

TABLE OF CONTENTS

FOREWORD

There are some people whose presence fills a room before they ever say a word. My sister Janice has always been one of those people.

All my life, she has been the standard, the one others measured themselves against, the one people noticed first, the one who didn't have to try to be seen because she simply was. Growing up, I learned early how this worked. Young men would come around, strike up a conversation with me, laugh a little too hard at my jokes, not because I was the destination, but because I was the pathway. As we used to say, they would "rub the cub to get to the bear." And the bear they were trying to reach was Janice; beautiful, confident, unforgettable.

And here is what is remarkable, time has not changed that. If anything, it has refined it. Even as she approaches seventy, she still, in every meaningful sense, is the prettiest woman in the room. But this book is not about surface beauty. It is about something deeper, something harder, and something far more enduring.

Janice's hair began to gray at an early age. It was in the DNA written into her story long before she had a say in it. We saw it in our parents, especially on our father's side. Growing up in the 1960s, our father made a different choice. He covered his gray, concealed it, managed it. But Janice chose another path. She did not hide it, she leaned into it, she wore it.

There is a powerful biblical passage in Hosea 7:9, where the prophet says, "Gray hairs are here and there upon him, yet he knoweth it not." It is a haunting image of change happening, so gradually, so quietly that one is unaware of it. Age, creeping unnoticed. Life, shifting beneath your feet while you are still convinced everything is the same.

Then there is the story often told of former First Lady Barbara Bush, whose hair turned gray overnight after the loss of a child. Barbara Bush's graying was a sudden, seismic transformation brought on by grief.

Janice's journey lives somewhere between those two realities. Not unaware like the man in Hosea. Not sudden like Barbara Bush, but steady, intentional, and conscious. Janice saw gray coming, and instead of resisting it, she received it. And that is where her courage lies.

Because let's be honest, gray hair is not just about hair, it's about what it represents. It's about time. It's about change. It's about the quiet fear many of us carry but rarely name, the fear of aging, of losing what once defined us, of becoming invisible in a world that worships youth. But Janice refuses invisibility. She teaches us that gray is not a surrender; it is a statement.

In these pages, she invites you into more than a hair journey. She invites you into a transformation of perspective. She speaks to the deeper work of self-care, self-love, and self-validation. The kind that does not depend on mirrors, compliments, or comparisons. The kind that comes from within.

I remember once asking an older woman how she was doing. She smiled and said, "My house is leaning, my foundation is squeaking, and there is a lot of snow on my roof. But I'm not disturbed, because I've committed myself to a lot of interior decorating."

That stayed with me. Because at some point in life, we all realize that the exterior will change. The roof will gather snow. The structure will shift. But the real question becomes: What have you done on the inside? This book is about interior decorating of the soul.

Janice will show you what it looks like to cultivate beauty that cannot fade, strength that cannot be shaken, and confidence that does not apologize for the passing of time. She reminds us that aging is not something to be feared; it is something to be embraced, interpreted, and even celebrated.

And if you walk with her through these pages, you may find yourself arriving at a place where you can say, with peace and power:

"There's snow on my roof aplenty; the living of life is the proof. But as long as there is fire in my furnace, I don't mind the snow on my roof."

This is not just poetry; this is freedom. And that is the gift my sister Janice offers you in this book.

INTRODUCTION

I have always wanted to write a book and knew that it would be about my gray hair. I remember reading the very first chapter I wrote of this book and weeping. Overcome with emotion, I was amazed that something, like my hair, had inspired me to write a book.

I have always known I had a story to share, but I thought people would think I was crazy if they asked me what my book was about, and I would respond that it was about my gray hair. I have to admit, my insecurities did get the best of me, and my first chapter sat on a computer longer than I anticipated.

My sons, Brandon and Zachary, earnestly and constantly encouraged me to finish my book. They didn't care what it was about. All they cared about was me, their mother, finishing something the masses needed to hear. My husband, Dean, and my sisters, Natalie and Sylvia, also encouraged me to finish this book. So, I finally gave in and sent my brother, Kevin, a copy of my first chapter. He's written many successful books, and I knew he would be honest with me about mine. But I wasn't sure what he would think about the chapter.

"Janice, this chapter is great!" Kevin said over the phone. "You've got something to say and a story to tell! So, why are you waiting to finish this? Stop procrastinating and get it done. You are an inspiration to so many, so why not share it with the world?"

I felt more hopeful and confident from the conversation and responded, "Okay, okay…I'll finish my book." But four years later, I still didn't have a finished book.

Looking back, I was so unsure of myself. I appreciated the support from my husband, sons, sisters, and brother, but I still wasn't sure whether what I had to say was of interest or value to the masses. My family believed in me and had faith in my abilities, but I needed to believe and have faith in myself to complete the book. And I am so happy to share that I finally completed this book about the wisdom from my gray hair.

CHAPTER ONE

The Birth of the Gray Head

You may be asking, "Why would anyone write a serious book about their hair?"

Well, before you judge me for what sounds like a mundane, trite, self-centered, and inconsequential literary waste of time, I ask that you hear me out.

No, this is not a book about the existential threat to our democracy or how to overcome global warming. Instead, this book is a serious– and sometimes funny– look into how something so simple– attached to my life– has taught me critical life lessons.

I believe that we are all looking for inspiration, whether it comes from the wisdom of men and women who came before us, or from a sports hero who sacrificed everything to win a gold medal. Sometimes inspiration looks different, like survival, overcoming, and even just standing still on your principles.

Often, we look outside ourselves for inspiration, which can take the form of searching for role models who reflect our own possibilities. Sometimes it looks like mentorship. Sometimes it looks like a friendship. And sometimes it's looking from afar at a woman or man standing in their truth.

Throughout my life, I have been inspired in so many ways by men and women who carried themselves with dignity even when life felt unfair. I've been inspired by people who have reinvented themselves, refused to give up, and fully stood up for their right to speak their truth without apology. Being inspired by amazing people has helped me see my own life, my own beauty, and my own evolution, slowly and unexpectedly, allowing me to discover that true inspiration has always been a part of my identity.

While writing this book at 69, I realized that one of my inspirations has been my hair. My GRAY hair. Yep, my kinky, curly, nappy, coily, zig-zag, sometimes relaxed, short, long, stubborn, and very temperamental gray hair follicles. As far as I can remember, there's never been a time in my life when I did not have gray hair. In elementary school, I had a few gray strands here and there. In high school, I had a few more. And by the time I got to college, I had "salt-and-pepper" hair.

Now, here I am– a full-fledged gray head– who has done her research as to why and how I got here. The human body has millions of hair follicles that line the skin and generate hair and color. From what I have gathered, I understand the science of going gray.

According to my research, Canities, the scientific term for graying hair, is a natural process caused by the progressive loss of pigment (melanin) from hair follicles, leading to gray hair. Canities can be influenced by many factors, including aging, genetics, stress, nutrition, autoimmune conditions, and the environment, with the only way to treat or restore pigmentation as of 2026 being through artificial dyes.

According to an article in Harper's Bazaar Magazine titled "Finding More Gray Hairs? You're Not Alone," Dr. Marie Hayag, a New York City board-certified dermatologist and founder of Fifth Avenue Aesthetics, linked genetic predisposition and environmental factors to the development of gray hair (Maril, 2020). Dr. Hayag explained that there isn't a set time for when premature graying occurs. Her studies show that White people can start graying as early as age 20, with Asians in second place, graying around age 25, and Black people graying at age 30 (Maril, 2020).

With so many factors that can cause gray hair, I don't know what happened in my body as a child that made my hair follicles stop producing pigment. But biologically, I guess that's what happened. And not to spill family secrets: I can put some blame on my parents for my gray hair.

Gray Roots

Let's take it all the way back to my parents and their gray hair. My Dad, Laken Cosby, Jr., had gray hair. Beautiful gray hair. But you never saw it because he used the men's hair coloring product *Great Day for Men* for years! Daddy is probably turning over in his grave knowing I am sharing his secret. Yes, Daddy dyed his hair and really thought no one knew– even though his overly dyed hair had started turning green. Yes– green! Or maybe Daddy just didn't know what the hell he was doing when he colored his hair. It was dark brown, with lime-green roots, and it made my very handsome father look older and rather *odd* about the head.

I never understood why Daddy didn't just embrace his gray. He would have looked so fine with it. Didn't they always say men with gray hair looked distinguished?

Well, it wasn't until 2006, when Daddy was in his late 70s, that he finally let his gray hair see the light of day. No more hair dye– and he looked so debonair.

Now, my Mom's story is a little different…

My Mom, Clora Elizabeth Cosby, was 36 when she passed away, and I was 12 years old. But I vividly remember her dark brown hair. I had two aunts who were beauticians, Great Aunt Betty on my mother's side, but it was Aunt Barbara or Aunt Barb, on my father's side, who would come to the house to style my sisters' hair, my hair, and my mother's hair. Mom had a beautiful head of hair, too, which my aunt would shampoo, cut, and color. But then Mom would do what I thought was the craziest thing. As soon as Aunt Barb finished styling Mom's hair, Mom would put her thick, dark brown, chin-length synthetic wig back on. Every day!

At the time, I didn't know, but secretly, at her very young age, Mom was graying too. And I believe the wig was really used to hide her gray hair. Back then, in the 1960s, women did everything to hide their gray hair because it was seen as old and unattractive. So every other week, my Aunt Barb covered Mom's beautiful gray hair with an auburn dye– and then Mom plopped that wig back on. Looking back, considering my gene pool, it was inevitable that I would have some gray strands.

Although my mom made questionable choices about her hair, she was a true fashionista. Her style and taste in clothes were impeccable, and I believe some of that had an impact on me.

I've always been intrigued by fashion and hair, and in particular, gray hair. I believe that hair choices make a statement about who we are. It doesn't tell the whole story, but it does give a glimpse into who a person is. It's like looking into someone's eyes or observing how a person walks or moves their hands while they talk. Growing up as a teen in the 1970s, I don't recall seeing Black women with gray hair. Beauty for Black women felt bold, expressive, and deeply tied to identity. I remember wearing my Afro and Afro puffs. That was my cool era, and I loved it. Hair wasn't just a style– it was culture. It was Black pride and closely connected to the Civil Rights Movement and the Black Power Movement. Black womanhood, as I saw it as a teen, looked strong and vibrant.

But even during the movement of uplifting Black beauty, something I don't remember seeing in the 70s was a Black woman with gray hair. Not my maternal grandmother, Clora Dean Miller, nor my paternal grandmother, Maudie Cosby. Not in magazines. Not on TV. Not in beauty ads. Gray hair was not viewed as beautiful or aspirational.

So, while Black womanhood in the 70s taught me pride as we were saying it loud: we were "Black and proud," and sporting huge Afros, Afro-puffs, and Dashikis, with our fists held high, I still didn't have the full timeline of Black beauty. That's why my gray hair feels bigger than me. It's not just personal. It's generational. It's expanding the image of what Black beauty looks like– not just at one stage of life, but throughout all of it.

Embracing My Roots

My parents, for some reason, thought it was important to hide their natural hair color. But when I think about why they may have dyed their hair, I don't think it was about vanity. I think it was about the times and the world they were navigating. For their generation, appearance was often tied directly to opportunity and respect.

Daddy owned Cosby Realty, a real estate company, located in the West End of Louisville, Kentucky, a predominantly African American part of town and community. Mom was the prominent pastor's daughter and a successful piano teacher. Back then, they were seen as a "power couple."

Aging, especially visibly aging in the 70s, could change how people treated you, how seriously you were taken, and even how secure you felt. My parents were coming of age during and after segregation and during a time when being seen as polished, professional, and "acceptable" could open doors that might otherwise be closed. Looking young and energetic, in the traditional understanding of attractiveness, wasn't just about beauty. It was about access. So, for Mom and Dad, hiding their natural gray hair was a necessity.

But I get it. Gray hair means different things to different people.

Take, for example, my hair journey. There have been times over the years when people have challenged me to color my hair for various reasons. I guess their reasoning was based on their own perspective on gray hair, which differed from my own. As mentioned earlier, gray hair has often been viewed as old, aged, hard to manage, unruly, and unattractive. And this is even more true when it comes to being in a relationship.

Before I was married to my husband, Dean, I was a single woman in the dating scene. It was 2015 when a girl friend of mine suggested I dye my hair. She was under the impression that men would see me as old, and I would be more attractive if the gray were gone. I still recall her words that echoed in my mind.

"Janice, you still have a pretty face, so why not dye it a soft brown? It'll make you look younger."

She meant well, but that fell on deaf ears as I brushed off her unsolicited advice. However, it did make me reevaluate the new dating world I was entering.

Over the years, my gray hair has been a topic of conversation not just with close friends and family, but wherever I go. Questions about my hair have come from many people– known and unknown, and places– public and personal. Yet all random encounters– at the grocery store checkout line, concerts, gyms, restaurants, Uber, and yes— in public restrooms– it gets *that* personal.

Occasionally, people want my entire hair regimen– my routine, hair products, the whole nine yards– and ask for suggestions. Many ask what hair color I use, and I politely explain that my hair is not bleached, dyed, or highlighted. It is naturally gray. These conversations emerge whether I'm by myself or with friends and family. And Lord knows, the interruptions from strangers with their comments about my hair have irritated my girl friends and my husband. Yet, when I'm asked questions about my hair, I'm not bothered or insulted. It just reminds me of my life story of how I've grown and overcome.

Gray is the Story of My Life

When I think about my gray hair, I see it as a story of my life. My ups and my downs. The struggles and triumphs. As I look at photos of myself over the years, I recognize each phase of my graying hair. Growing more seasoned with each season. And by the phase of my gray hair in photos, I can tell you what was going on in my life. When I was salt-and-pepper, I was pregnant with my first child and preparing to give birth. And when I was almost completely gray, I was vice president at a national health care system. I have experienced many changes in my life, just as my hair has changed color.

I've experienced many challenges, as we all have. Marriage. Divorce. Loneliness. Self-doubt. Life can be inconsistent. Crazy and full of unexpected events. However, my gray hair has been the most consistent aspect of my life. This gray hair of mine has been with me through thick and thin. It's been my best friend. And even though it has changed over the years, it never lets me down.

My gray hair has given me the strength to be me– the real me. It has allowed me to grow old gray-fully. My hair has taught me to be proud and to present myself in a professional work environment that does not always embrace aging women and men. I mean, think about it, when was the last time you've seen a woman running a company or in an executive position with gray hair? Not many, I'm sure.

I admit that in this very visual, instant-gratification, look-alike world, gray hair may not be aesthetically pleasing to some and is synonymous with getting old. But if that's the case, I've been old my entire life. However, despite what many believe about gray hair, over the years, my gray hair has taught me that I am still attractive and sexy, and so are the many other gray heads in the world.

"So, what does growing old gracefully mean?" I'm glad you asked.

But to be honest, I don't know how to answer that question entirely. I just know my story and that I want to grow in grace.

Now, at my tender-seasoned age, I understand that my gray strands are a metaphor for my life: strong, stand out, wiry, dry, at times coarse and rough, but most times manageable– and constantly growing. Very textured, but always shining through. And that, my friend, is why this is a serious book about hair.

CHAPTER TWO

Living in the Gray

The word "gray" is often used to describe something in between. It's neither black nor white, so it exists in what we call the "gray" area. We use that metaphor all the time to describe situations that feel indefinite, unsure, or hard to explain. Gray can also represent a train of thought or an opinion that doesn't land firmly on one side or the other. It becomes a convenient alternative when there's no clear or easy explanation.

To be a gray head carries much of that same connotation.

Being gray can place you in an in-between space. It forces you to step outside of your comfort zone and challenge the way people see you, and sometimes how you see yourself. It invites assumptions and curiosity, often before you open your mouth. But if you are willing to accept it, being gray also allows you to experience an alternative way of living and a different way of being seen.

Later in life, I would learn that the grayer I became, the more those gray strands would teach me valuable lessons I never imagined learning.

Graying Early and Acceptance.

In my 30s, I was a young wife and mother with a degree in Public Relations, and a professional career in healthcare marketing that was just beginning. During that time, my gray hair didn't feel like a statement. I just viewed my hair as just that– hair. I didn't see it as anything special. It didn't feel political, cultural, or even intentional. It was simply part of me. I wasn't trying to stand out or blend in– I was just living my life, raising my boys, and moving through the world the best way I knew how.

But gray has a way of making you visible, whether you want it to or not.

Being gray invites questions. It draws attention. And it often challenges people's expectations– especially when it doesn't line up with the rest of who you are. Gray hair doesn't always fit neatly into societal boxes. Many view people with gray hair as old, wise, outdated, out of touch, retired, or near retirement and not quite with it. Unfortunately, for some reason, gray hair is not often viewed as a sign of youthfulness, energy, and vitality. But that's not at all how I view gray hair.

Living in the gray has taught me how to be comfortable with ambiguity. I have learned to exist in spaces where I did not quite fit, and instead of shrinking, I have learned to stand tall. Gray taught me that you can be different and still belong. And over time, I realized that gray wasn't just about my hair, but it was about how I navigated my life.

Young and Gray

Some of the most important people in my life have been my girl friends. Over the years, especially in my 30s and 40s, I have often been the only girl friend in my crew with gray hair and have stood out like a sore thumb. And I admit, I was a bit uncomfortable back then.

I truly loved the look of my gray hair. I loved how it was growing in. But was it really "OK" for me to love it? I mean, no one else my age had gray hair. *Is something wrong with me because I chose not to dye it? I wondered.*

But even then, not one girl friend put pressure on me to dye my hair, so the issue and the insecurity were within me. And I did go through a phase when I wanted to blend in and have the same color hair as my friends.

Sometimes I wondered what my hair would look like if I changed its color. What would I look like with auburn, dark brown, or even golden blonde hair? Would my girl friends eventually get tired of having the old, gray-haired lady hanging out with them? So why not test it out?

Well, one day, when I was 39, I decided to take the plunge. I've always said that if I were going to dye my gray hair, my color of choice would be auburn. I love auburn-colored hair, and I thought it would look good on me. So, one day, I went shopping at the wig outlet and found a cute auburn wig. It was cut in a page-boy type style. I wore it to work the next day, and to my surprise, the reaction was not what I expected.

First of all, nobody recognized me. Everyone thought I looked strange, and one person asked if I was sick. I was very uncomfortable with my new artificial hair, but I managed to get through the eight hours on the job. Later that evening, I was scheduled to have dinner with two girlfriends. This was my big chance to introduce them to the new look. Their reactions were similar to those of my co-workers. Shock and awe. Silence. Then the question, "Why?"

My girl friends told me I didn't need to wear a wig and that being a gray-haired Janice was the *authentic* Janice. The Janice they loved. They both agreed that my gray hair was a part of what made me– well, me. After our brief but significant discussion, I went to the ladies' room, took off my wig, fixed my hair as best I could, and then proudly walked back to the table with my girl friends. We all laughed!

That day, I learned that yes, I am different. And that's okay.

That was my *in the gray* moment. Most of our days are filled with decisions that aren't clearly right or wrong. There are many areas of life that fall into the gray, as very little is absolute. Relationships, careers– so many components of life can exist in the gray. Mine certainly did. And my beginnings also began in the gray.

At times, we think life is a straight line and should go as *we* planned. But that's not realistic— well, at least, it hasn't been realistic for me. Very little in my life has gone as planned. And to be honest, I'm not sure I've had a specific plan. But I've learned that life's most meaningful growth happens when things don't go as initially planned. When the relationship ends, the promotion doesn't come, and when the role you thought you would play in someone's life suddenly changes. Just like gray hair, gray seasons don't ask for permission. They just happen. So living in the gray taught me flexibility, self-trust, and the art of letting go.

Living in the Gray as a Mom

Believe it or not, being gray taught me to be a better mom.

Back in the 80s, when I was a younger mother, my sons, Brandon and Zachary, who are five years apart, have only seen me with salt-and-pepper or gray hair their whole lives. When my sons were toddlers, I was salt-and-pepper, and to me, my hair was just a beautiful mane. I was cute and still looked young, which was all that mattered to me at the time.

By the time my sons were teenagers, and more guidance and patience were critical, I was a gray head almost in full bloom. This was the season of exhaustion. However, I cherished every bit of my life as a young mother.

And come to think of it, I believe I was the only mom among my children's friends' mothers with gray hair. None of the other moms had gray hair except me, well, at least gray hair that was visible and uncovered. I clearly stood out at the Parent Teacher Conference meetings and at Zachary's and Brandon's basketball and football games, sitting in the bleachers. Fortunately, Brandon and Zachary learned at an early age the power of looking different, standing out, and being authentic.

Now, it's important to note that Brandon, Zachary, and their friends never treated me like the "old mom" because of my gray hair. To my boys, I was the fly mom, celebrated for my youthfulness, sassiness, and confidence. Being a gray-haired mom was who I was. It was my identity, and it was celebrated not just by me but by the people I loved most.

The gray hair strands that grew as my sons grew older were not just a sign of time passing. Each gray strand I earned was a marker of a season and a record of motherhood. But don't get me wrong. Gray doesn't necessarily mean an older age or the process of aging. While many believe that having children can "age you," or cause one to gray faster, that was not the case for me. I don't think I grayed fast because of my sons. I went gray because I *loved*. I loved my boys fiercely and worried silently, learning to be strong even when I felt unsure, and to let go when I wanted to hold on. This love has led to my gray hair.

Even losing my mother at age 12, I believe, forced me to learn strength long before I understood what strength really meant. At that age, you're still supposed to be someone's baby girl and have someone to run to when life feels too heavy and big. But when Mom passed, I didn't just lose her love and guidance. I lost the safety net that held me close and held our family together. Everything dramatically changed, so I had to learn to be strong. That early loss shaped everything about me, including my identity as a mother.

My mom, at age 36, left behind four children: my sister, Pam; me; my brother, Kevin; and my younger sister, Sylvia. Losing Mom planted a quiet, persistent fear inside of me– the fear that I might leave my own children too soon. For years, I carried an unspoken anxiety about dying early, about my children feeling the same emptiness I felt from losing my mother. But I had to let go of the idea that my Mom's story would repeat itself through me. Today, I now understand that every gray strand on my head represents blessed years of life– years my Mom didn't get to have. My gray hair is not just about aging. It's my symbolic badge of survival.

Motherhood is not about perfection, but about presence. At every stage of being a young mom, my hair changed along with me. It was as if my body was keeping score of every lesson I learned as a mother. My gray strands are my timeline.

As a young mom, being gray taught me that it's okay not to have everything figured out. Raising two sons shaped my body, my spirit, and my sense of self. Gray hair taught me humility when I made mistakes and permitted me to evolve without explanation, even when I knew the questions from people around me would keep coming. Living in the gray taught me courage when I didn't fit the mold.

Breaking the Mold

For centuries, social conditioning has taught us that beauty is youth, flawless skin, thinness, and perfection. From magazines to movies, from commercials to social media filters, we see the same message over and over again: fight and hide aging. And the messaging doesn't just live on billboards, in music videos, or movie screens. The message is also in daily conversations about desirability, relevance, and visibility.

According to American beauty standards, gray hair does not fit the universal mold of beauty, especially on women. This is plain as day in the professional sector. Take, for instance, during my years as a healthcare executive, I never had gray-haired female colleagues. Not one. Just me. So, yes, while my gray hair didn't fit the mold, I learned to stand firm in an environment that didn't embrace gray hair. However, it wasn't until I began attending professional events years later that I started to see more women with gray hair, which was intriguing. I also noticed that when many of my female colleagues retired, they let their hair go gray. But why? Why wait so long to go gray? Unfortunately, social norms and standards, especially the media, teach us at an early age that beauty is directly connected to youth and must be protected at all costs.

Growing up, the myth that gray hair makes women look tired, neglected, washed-out, or old seemed true. There were so many commercials encouraging women to color their hair. Meanwhile, men were praised and labeled "distinguished" for having gray hair. As a result, hair dye became a sort of armor– not always worn for ourselves, but for the comfort of others. For the job interview. For the big date. For the 20th high school reunion. And even for the wedding.

But gray hair refuses to pretend and hide under a darker shade, which prevents it from fitting into society's unrealistic and unattainable beauty standards. Essentially, I believe gray hair makes people uncomfortable. It's uncomfortable because it refuses to pretend that time isn't passing and that life hasn't been lived. For many, when someone shows up gray, it represents letting go of youth and stepping outside of a social "approval system." I mean, realistically, whether we like it or not, graying *does* say that we are aging out loud– in front of everyone– for the whole world to see. And there lies the problem. Do we want people to see us age in full view?

My gray hair tells my truth– that Janice lives a full life. Choosing to wear my gray hair is *not* just a matter of style. It is a quiet rebellion. You didn't know my gray hair was rebellious, did you? My gray hair is a peaceful protest. It says, I will not erase myself to be accepted. It says, I honor who I have become and who I am becoming. Breaking the mold doesn't always have to be loud or dramatic, either. Sometimes it may look like standing in front of the mirror and deciding not to hide your authentic features. Other times, it may look like walking into a room knowing your hair tells a story before you ever speak. And it also may look like a woman who has stopped apologizing for her age. And maybe that's where quiet rebellion begins– in a simple decision to show up exactly as we are.

In many spaces, my gray hair is often viewed as a bold statement– not because it is extreme, but because it is honest. Women of all shades, ages, and walks of life have told me how much they admire me for wearing my gray hair.

Over the years, I have seen a shift in how people think about gray hair. It's been a long time coming, but gray hair is finally becoming more acceptable and embraced. Internationally, more women are choosing visibility over disguise. Gray hair is even beginning to grace the covers of magazines with admiration, no matter the age. Even on social media, many women of all ages are coloring or bleaching their hair gray or embracing their natural gray. It's become fashionable, refined, cool, chic, and elegant. I'm not going to call it a movement just yet, but I see it more often. So, yes, gray hair is shifting toward being seen as more desirable, and I love it! The appreciation and celebration of gray hair are showing up and showing out, revealing to my younger sisters that they don't need to fear aging or see themselves as lacking value, causing them to fade with time.

I talk to younger women whom I affectionately refer to as "youngins" about this very topic a lot. They often stop to ask me what hair dye I use to get my hair so silver. And I just love it when they ask because I can proudly tell them that my hair is naturally gray. Living in my truth puts a smile on my face, knowing that I've been cool and chic for years– on my terms! So, I'm encouraged and empowered by the collective embrace of gray hair from all ages.

See, this cultural shift is not just for the gray-haired but for women of all ages. Gray hair expands the timeline of relevance, beauty, and influence, acknowledging what was once hidden as openly appreciated and respected for its natural authenticity.

CHAPTER THREE

Gray, Power, and the Price of Visibility

I'll be the first to admit that early in my career, I didn't see many gray-haired women at the Corporate or C-suite level. Take, for example, Presidents, Vice-Presidents, or Directors. How many gray-headed men and women have you seen at that level? And when is the last time we've had a gray-haired president of the United States? Catching my drift? Now, President Obama did start graying, and it was visible! He seemed to embrace his gray, too. However, I see more White men wearing their gray hair than any other ethnicity or gender.

Now, you may be asking, "Jan, are you trying to ruin my career path? What exactly are you saying?"

Relax– I'm not trying to ruin your career path. I'm trying to make sure you don't spend 30 years building a career that requires you to hide who you are to keep it. And I get it. Men with gray hair do seem to get away with it more often, described as experienced, powerful, and wise. But it does make sense since we live in a historically White, male-dominated world that has led to this double standard. Just think about the times you have seen a man with gray hair in an executive position. They are often CEOs, judges, doctors, and professors– the representation of leadership. The truth of the matter is that men are just not targeted the same way women are when it comes to gray hair.

Yes, it's not fair. And yes, gray hair is still perceived by some as being "old."

Perhaps, you're thinking, "Until I reach my ultimate career level, I'll keep dyeing my hair." That's valid. And honestly, I understand that choice. I'm not here to judge. But I also believe something else to be true. I believe that going gray– for both women and men– can signal leadership, authenticity, and courage. I believe you can prove to the world that gray does not equate to old, outdated, or irrelevant. It's regal, sophisticated, and elegant. However, there have been times when I felt somewhat insecure and out of place with my gray hair. And the workplace environment has often been the setting for that test.

Stigma in the workplace

In 2014, I served as a state-wide Chief Marketing Officer for a national health care system. During that time, I participated in countless professional conferences and was unstoppable. I knew my work. I knew my industry. As I knew, I belonged in any space I walked into. However, while there was nothing out of the ordinary about any of the national conferences I attended, one in particular, in Chicago, Illinois, stands out as being monumental.

The opening session was bright and early at 9 am with more than 500 culturally diverse marketing and communications professionals from across the country. I walked into the large, cold, air-conditioned room with my heavy sweater ready for the frigid air. I was excited about the conference and eagerly anticipated the keynote speaker, someone I had researched weeks before traveling. And I admit that, though I was happy to represent my health system at this prestigious conference, I was a little bored by the roundtable discussion. So, inevitably, my mind wandered, and that's when my gaze and perspective of that room shifted from stepping into that room with all the confidence in the world to feeling a tinge of insecurity.

Looking around, the room was filled with young to middle-aged White professionals, with a sprinkling of people of color, all well-dressed in job-interview-ready, appropriate attire, with hair colors ranging from highlighted blonde, brunette, brown to jet black. As everyone sat at attention, upright and engaged in the moment, I immediately felt small and out of place in a sea of other well-respected professionals.

Is everyone staring at me? I wondered. *Have they been whispering and saying mean things about me?* These questions swarmed my mind and spun me in that oversized auditorium-style room.

My palms, sweating. My heart, pounding through my chest. I had never experienced hyperventilation before that day. *What the heck is going on with me?* I wondered.

Breathe, I coached myself silently. Taking in a few deep breaths.

Am I having a panic attack? I wondered, scanning the room again. *But why? Could the panic attack have come from being the only Black woman in the room? No. Been there and done that.*

But in that moment, being in that room felt different, like there was a spotlight on me. Like I was a frog being dissected under a microscope in a seventh-grade biology class. Well, at least from my fragile perspective, that's how it felt. And it certainly wasn't my blackness. That wasn't what triggered my distress.

But then something else registered, and I realized the difference. I was the only gray head in the room. And that realization stopped me cold.

Immediately following my bout of self-loathing and feelings of inadequacy, my inner critic started to take over while I was seated in the padded conference room chair.

Then, another thought came to mind. *How does my boss see me? How do the people in the room see me?* Some of my co-workers were also attending the conference.

Do they see me as old? Do my colleagues see me as out of touch because of my gray hair? Am I relevant? Will I be promoted? Will my appearance affect my chances for growth or advancement? Will my colleagues consider my perspective outdated or less relevant because of my gray hair?

All of these questions– and uncertainties– swirled in my mind. I was a mess as this was my first experience of feeling insecure about my gray hair at work.

The highly anticipated keynote speaker was next on the agenda, and I really wanted to hear her presentation, but my nerves were all over the place. I was fidgety and couldn't keep still in my seat. And quite frankly, I was getting very irritated with myself.

What happened to the confident Jan? Where did she go? I was in a sea of polished, confident professionals who seemed so sure of their place in the room. But at that moment, I forgot who I was. I was old and small, and shrank into invisibility, becoming an observer, not a participant, and the confident Jan who believed she deserved to be there. I no longer blended in but stood out, terrified.

Before this, I was feeling very confident and had come to slay! I was immaculately dressed in my cobalt blue designer business suit, Jimmy Choo pumps, and my Chanel bag. Heck, I was a supermodel, Vogue cover-ready (*two snaps*)! But that was before I stepped into that conference room. Now, here I was, feeling like a has-been, overwhelmed and ultimately devastated.

Desperate to pull myself together and regain my super-power, I decided to step out of the room for a moment, grab water, and collect myself. I needed a reset. Standing up to rescue myself from the malaise, I whispered, "Excuse me" at least 50 times, making my way through the empty, narrow aisle, enclosed by hundreds of blank faces.

Why did I have to sit in the third row that day?

Trying not to draw any more attention to myself than I already had, I walked to the back of the auditorium and stood quietly alone in the doorway, waiting for the speaker to finish.

Feeling uncomfortable as the only one standing there, I decided to sneak out the door and made my way to the ladies' lounge– a place of refuge– thank God. I needed to chill for a bit.

Walking into the lounge, two beautiful pink chaise lounge chairs called out to me to take a seat. But then, my nerves kicked in again, leading me to think, *what if a colleague came in and saw me luxuriating in the women's lounge when I should be in the opening session*? To mitigate any potential misperceptions, I went into a restroom stall for privacy, then made my way back to the sink area. Washing my hands, I admired the stunning, tall, wide mirrors above the individual sinks, illuminated on both sides by vanity lights made for a movie star's dressing room in Hollywood. And that's when I looked into the mirror at the woman staring back at me– gray-headed me.

Why am I the only one in that huge auditorium with gray hair? I mumbled to the woman in the mirror. *Why am I freaking out about this today*– in Chicago? Well, thankfully, no one was in the restroom. I'm sure if someone had seen me staring at myself and mumbling, they would have been concerned. Yet, and still, I didn't have an answer, so I headed back to the main hallway to the conference room. Before I went into the auditorium, to clear my head of my remaining doubt, I stopped to get a bottle of water and gulped it down. *Okay, I'm dehydrated. Maybe that's my problem*? I thought.

Walking down the long, wide, paisley-carpeted hallway, I stood outside the auditorium's massive, double doors, where I noticed a young woman I had seen during the coffee break in another area of the convention center. She stood out, looking fly in her gorgeous wrap dress and fabulous boots. As the only two people standing in the hallway waiting to enter, it was only natural that we start a conversation with introductions at least.

I shared with her that I loved her ensemble, to which she smiled and thanked me. The woman's hair was a sandy color with rich brown highlights. Her face was very tan, and her sculpted, dramatic cheekbones had the dramatic silhouette of Angelina Jolie. Then, with a look of satisfaction and admiration, she said, "I love your hair. It's so becoming on you."

I was flattered and thanked her.

Then, she said something that felt like an epiphany. Leaning in slightly, she confessed, "You know, most of the women in that room have gray hair just like you–but they cover it up." And then she lifted her blonde bangs to show me her gray roots.

"See?" she laughed. "I'm too chicken to show my gray. But under this, I'm as gray as you are. But my gray would never look as fabulous as yours."

I accepted the lovely compliment, and we both laughed. But what the lady said next resonated deeply with me.

"I know I just met you," she began, "but you have truly inspired me. Seeing you being your authentic self has encouraged me. You have given me something to think about, and maybe one day I'll be brave enough to show my gray, too."

In that moment, something inside of me shifted: visibility has a price, but it also has power.

Visibility and the Power Within You

While being seen can mean being judged, it can also mean being noticed by the people who need to see you the most.

Since my experience at the conference in Chicago, I have learned that leadership isn't just about titles or positions. Sometimes leadership looks like simply showing up as yourself in spaces not designed with you in mind.

As I reflect on that experience, I now understand that gray hair didn't make me insecure that day. I was merely reacting to what I felt gray hair possibly meant to the other people in that room. Perhaps, like many, they believe youth is more valuable than wisdom, that beauty has an expiration date, and that maturity and gray hair should be hidden. But in my opinion, that's not true.

Reflecting on my experience in that conference room, I had forgotten to own the best parts of me. The unseen parts.

Strong.

Intelligent.

Full of wisdom.

Confident.

Mature.

Resilient.

Kind-hearted.

Authentic. *Those parts.*

Looking back over my life, I have come to learn that I am so much more than a gray-haired woman.

And once I remembered that, I let the insecurity go.

CHAPTER FOUR

Dating While Gray

Dating. *Oh boy.*

The moment you say the word, you can almost feel the pressure, especially when you're gray-headed in a very competitive, image-driven world. Immediately, the thought creeps in: *I must dye this gray out of my hair to even have a fighting chance.*

So, let's have a real, honest conversation about dating prospects for a gray head.

I've never dyed my hair. That means most of my dating– and married– life, I've been gray. Well, actually, that's not entirely true. There was a brief moment in my life when I decided to try something different. This was in 1981, when my hair was salt-and-pepper, and I thought my "new boo," who had seen my natural hair color, might like me better with a so-called "younger look" about the head.

Let me be clear– I did not know what I was doing.

But I have always been brave, which led me to spray my naturally salt-and-pepper hair with auburn color, followed by peroxide. And not salon peroxide– oh no. I used the bottle of peroxide sitting in my medicine cabinet for wound care. Can you believe that? I looked crazy! But I tried to make it work because I thought it would help keep my "new boo." Talk about insecurity!

But his reaction helped ease my mind. As he walked me from my house to his car, he actually told me he liked it– the new crazy color. Well, his reaction did make me feel vindicated for trying something new.

At dinner, we talked about aging and how we imagined ourselves growing older. Larry was a little older than me and constantly spoke about traveling after retirement, having grandkids, and sitting on the beach. He nicknamed me "Red." Larry often called me "Red" because when I got excited, nervous, or anxious, my face would turn red, which gave rise to the nickname.

During dinner, Larry said, "Red, you are going to age well if you stay true to yourself and drink a lot of water." I must admit that Larry's advice has stayed with me— even though at times I fall short of staying true to myself. But I do drink a LOT of water!

He had a great sense of humor and focused on living a healthy life. He had a way of always keeping me at ease, and I was pleased that my new hairstyle was a hit. Changing my hair color was a big adjustment for me, and I wasn't sure if *I* even liked it. But if *he* liked it, I should *love* it. *Right?* At that point during our dinner, I remember thinking, *Wow, Larry must really love my auburn-peroxide hair*. Even though it had been on my mind before arriving at the restaurant, it was becoming less of a factor as Larry carried on.

Then, Larry said something I did not expect.

"Red, I really love your salt-and-pepper hair. I can even visualize how beautiful you will be at age 50, 60, and even 70. It's so becoming on you. It's sexy, and you glow with confidence, and you certainly stand out in a crowd. It fits your spirit, and it's authentically you! Plus, you don't need to change your hair color, for me, or for anyone– unless it's something YOU really want to change."

My jaw hit the ground. I was so surprised and never imagined someone saying that, better yet, my boo.

After all these years, that moment has stayed with me.

I'm not saying all men love gray hair. But I can honestly say I haven't met one man who was turned off by it. And if we fast-forward to 2026, gray hair is fascinating– and yes, sexy– to many men of all backgrounds. See, while some women believe that men see gray hair as old, that's not always the case. In fact, gray hair often brings out the best in our natural complexions and facial features because it's natural and authentic.

Gray Hair and Boredom

Now, let me say this clearly– if you want to mix it up a little, there's nothing wrong with that. There are many ways to try new hair colors and styles without doing what I did to my gray hair– applying hair color *AND* peroxide. Instead, buy a wig. Get a blonde one. A red one. Heck, get a blue one. Live a little.

When you hit 50 and above, you may feel pressure to change your hair color if you find yourself with some gray strands, whether it is to compete with younger women, fit in with women around your age who don't have gray hair, or date again.

As a gray head, I encourage you to stick with the gray. But if you choose to go in a different direction, it's understandable.

Just know this– sometimes when you're gray and try to cover it, it could potentially make you look older. Gray hair is hard to color because it lacks pigment and natural oils, making its cuticle or outer layer coarser and more resistant than your natural hair texture, preventing dye from penetrating easily. Because of this, coloring the gray often requires specialized techniques, such as using a more potent chemical to open the cuticle for color. It takes a very dark permanent dye to cover gray hair. For instance, dark color applied to gray hair can look very harsh, unnatural, and sometimes a little bit crazy. And when gray hair starts growing out around the roots, it can look a little *skunkish.*

So, bottom line, over 50 and gray is very sexy. You CAN rock it on a date– and all the way to the altar.

Swiping Left or Right in the Gray

Now, let's talk about online dating.

Please– do not post a photo of yourself with a completely different hair color from your actual hair color, as this is disingenuous and a false representation of your current appearance. That's like a man posting a photo saying he's 6'2" when he's really 5'7."

It's misleading.

If someone is going to meet you through a photo on a dating site, let them meet you as you are, currently. Not a version of you that doesn't exist anymore or never has. Authenticity matters and honestly is freeing.

The reality is, gray hair doesn't need defending. It doesn't need explaining, and it definitely doesn't need fixing. It needs owning. So, own it, sis!

Here's a funny story.

My good childhood friend, Howard, whom I grew up with in Louisville, Kentucky, is a kind gentleman with a wonderful family whom I loved very much– "Buster," his older brother, parents, and sisters. The Stikes family was like a second family to me, and

Howard was like a brother. He was my sounding board and friend who looked after me.

However, over the years, as adults, Howard and I lost contact once I moved to Detroit, Michigan, in 1984, got married, and had my two sons. But sometimes, when I would go home to Louisville for a visit, Howard would come to my home church, St. Stephen Baptist Church, where my grandfather had pastored for 40 years and where my brother, Kevin, has been the pastor for over 45 years. So, when Howard would pop in on a Sunday at church just to see me, it was always a special day.

Fast forward: years later, Howard and I lost contact again, until I attended the Annual Mackinac Policy Conference at the historic Grand Hotel on Mackinac Island, Michigan. *Thee* Mackinac Policy Conference–which is a big deal for professionals worldwide invested in growing Michigan's economy. I loved going to that conference, connecting with friends and colleagues, and hearing excellent speakers.

In May of 2016, I attended the conference, sitting in a seminar with 60 people in a small room, when halfway through the presentation, my cell phone started buzzing. Looking down at my phone, Howard's name popped up.

Wow, I thought. *I haven't heard from Howard in a long time. I wonder if everything's ok.*

Deciding to let the call go to voicemail, I put my phone back in my purse and returned to my notes to see where the speaker was in the presentation. But about 10 minutes later, my phone buzzed again. It was Howard calling back. Now, I'm thinking, *this is getting interesting. What could be so urgent that he called back again within 10 minutes?* Curiosity got the best of me, so I decided to take a break and step outside to feel the rays of sunshine on my face and call Howard back. As soon as I stepped outside into the beautiful sunlight, I heard the clackety-clack of horses, so I knew a carriage was approaching. To get to Mackinac Island, you have to ride the ferry, and while there, the only modes of transportation are horse-drawn carriages and bicycles, since cars are not allowed. Jumping in the carriage, I settled into the comfortable, cushioned seat as my coachman transported this *queen* around the island– it was so me, right? Anyway– I digress.

Returning Howard's call, he immediately answered.

"Janice, how are you?" he asked. But before I could respond, he quickly interrupted me.

"We can catch up later, but I want you to know that I've been divorced for a while, and I've joined the online dating app Match.com."

At that time, I didn't know much about online dating, so I was very confused why Howard was calling me about a dating app.

Then, Howard said, "I was swiping right… and then your photo popped up! And I'm certain it was you. I think it was a photo of you from a magazine. You have on a red dress, and you've got your hand on your hip.

It's a beautiful picture of you, but I was wondering why you are on this app, and I know that you are married."

I was flabbergasted and speechless!

Then, Howard continued, "After I read the woman's name and her profile, I realized it was someone impersonating you. The woman said she was from Louisville, still lived here, and was 45 years old." Growing up together as childhood friends, Howard knew my age, which further caught him off guard, leading him to figure out that someone had stolen my identity!

What???

I was appalled. But I did smile when Howard told me the imposter had me at 45 years old. *Sweet!*

While riding around the island in my royal horse-drawn carriage, Howard encouraged me to reach out to Match.com and request that they remove the profile because someone was using my likeness.

Again– *the nerve*!

I thanked Howard, and we promised to stay in touch before saying our good-byes, bringing my horse-drawn carriage ride to an end and before I knew it, I was back at the conference building. However, while in my seat, I couldn't help but wonder whether I should see the impersonation as a compliment or a violation, and I just couldn't stop thinking about it for the rest of the conference.

Ultimately, when I returned home, I did reach out to the dating app, and, as I requested, according to Howard, Match.com removed the fake profile.

I'm not sure why someone used my photo in their profile, but I can't blame them. I mean, it *is* one of my favorite photos. But– even so, it did give me pause. *Why would someone use the photo of a 60-something-year-old woman with gray hair and say they are 45? For online dating?*

No Filters. No Fiction.

I'm still perplexed by Howard's discovery to this day.

Although I've never experienced online dating, I do believe that it can tempt you to become a fictional character. Anyone can create a profile that bears a slight resemblance or a complete falsification of someone's actual appearance. We can all be critical about how we look on a particular day, our hair, and our body type. But I believe that if I have to disguise myself to get a date, I'm already on the wrong date.

Authenticity is the ultimate superpower move for both women and men. No matter your hair color, your body type, or the sound of your laugh– showing up as yourself saves time *and* heartbreak. I may not be everyone's type with my gray hair. But I *am* someone's type. Most importantly, I am *my* type. And you know, there is something bold and powerful about putting your *real* face on the internet and declaring, "This is me." No apology.

Online dating is not about perfection. You can make a connection without a disguise. Let your profile photos match who you really are. Let your words sound like your voice. If you are 5'2, own it. If you are 190 pounds, own it. If you are 69, own it. And if your hair is gray or any other color, own it. No matter your age, shape, shade, or stage, you are always in style.

Dating while gray isn't about lowering your standards or hiding who you are. It's about showing up fully confident, honest, and comfortable in your own skin.

And that, more than anything else, is attractive.

CHAPTER FIVE

A Lesson in Freedom

Over the years, my hair, which refuses to adapt, has taught me to be free. You can't hold gray hair captive. You can't lock it down. It's loud, bold, and audacious. Gray hair does what it wants. It has its own rhythm, is hard to control, and constantly yearns to be free. I've learned that freedom comes from not trying to control everything. And that's why I believe my gray hair has helped me step forward, become more visible, and feel more confident.

For years, I believed control was synonymous to confidence. If I could manage my appearance, I could manage how I was perceived. If I could keep my gray hair smooth and shape it without a fuss, my life would be much easier. But control is exhausting. Every hair relaxer or root touch-up becomes a chore and a deadline. You *may* be familiar with that deadline if you have relaxed hair. It's the day when new hair growth and relaxed gray hair strands meet, and you feel you can't go another day without getting a touch-up! And it comes with a price, too. Every mirror is a judgment and a performance review.

Constantly trying to control my uncontrollable hair was becoming like a second job. I genuinely love my gray hair, but I was putting way too much pressure on myself to make sure it looked appropriate to the masses. I tried to control the curl pattern. I tried to control the texture. I wanted to make it soft, and not so coarse. But I began to realize that my gray hair was longing to be free, which birthed *my gray spiky pixie.*

I have long since become accustomed to my hair's personality of doing what it wants and not what I say. And I've learned to be okay with that. My spiky pixie is free. It steps out of line. It breaks all the rules and firmly refuses to lie down. But I have to admit that I have *much respect* for my hair—it's strong and can never be duplicated. I give my gray hair *mad respect.*

Being gray has opened doors for me. Doors I never imagined would open. Because I started graying at a very young age and my look was classy and sophisticated, it attracted attention from professionals across various business sectors and organizations, magazines, and social spaces I never sought out.

When I moved to Michigan, I tried so many different hair stylists, and none knew how to take care of gray hair. Oftentimes, I would leave the salon with my hair looking so whack! My gray hair would turn out a bright blue, yellowish-gray, and so over-processed that my hair would start to break off. I was so frustrated with one stylist that I walked out of the salon with soaking wet hair. But thankfully, soon thereafter, a friend told me about a stylist who *really* knew how to take care of gray heads like mine. Thank God for Jacqui Martin!

Now, let's talk about national recognition for a gray head.

As my hairstylist for almost 20 years, Jacqui was an amazing, beautiful soul. However, sadly, Jacqui passed away a few years ago. But her memory still lives on with me.

Jacqui loved styling my hair. But she was more than a stylist. She was my friend, bootleg therapist, cheerleader, and prayer partner. And Jacqui *loved* to talk. And she talked very fast, even while cutting your hair, which could be a little concerning sometimes, but she never made a mistake. Jacqui loved setting the mood at the hair salon, and music was always playing. And if you were down and feeling low, she would offer you her secret champagne stash to lift your spirits. I would stop in her salon for conversations and, without an appointment, have her cut or style my hair. Nothing was off the table for discussion– family, politics, our children, fashion, and, of course, dating and marriage. We had fun together.

One day, in 2012, while getting my hair done, Jacqui asked, "Jan, have you seen this magazine?"

Jacqui held up a copy of *MORE* Magazine, a popular national women's magazine created by the Meredith Corporation in New York City. In 2010, the magazine introduced the annual *MORE* Beauty Search Contest, open to women over 30, offering cash prizes and the chance to be featured in the magazine. This prominent competition was designed to highlight beauty unrestricted by age. The magazine's goal was to redefine beauty standards by showcasing women with experience, poise, and confidence, rather than focusing solely on youth. Thousands of women participated in the contest each year.

"Yes, I've seen it," I responded. "I actually have a subscription."

Jacqui continued, "So, did you see the info about the Ageless Beauty contest? The contest ends in a few weeks, and I think you should enter. I believe you can win."

Jacqui continued, "They have age categories, and I saw the pictures of last year's winners, and I know that you could win or be a finalist because you look much younger than your age."

I truly thought that Jacqui was just humoring me. But the more she talked, the more I could tell she was *very* serious which led to the next thought, *Why not?* Jacqui had always had my best interest at heart, so why was I questioning her judgment now? But of course, a little insecurity set in— plus, I had never been in any type of beauty contest before. But Jacqui was convinced that if I entered, I would win, so I at least considered the idea.

"But Jacqui, what about my hair?" I asked. The past winners are very youthful, and I think my gray hair would be a turnoff. I'm just not sure." Nervously, I flipped through the magazine and noticed that most of the women in the photo ads and articles were White, around 40-50 years old, very tall, and thin.

Well, that definitely ain't me, I thought. I had no idea what the judges were looking for.

Jacqui had a couple of photos of me on her station from previous hairstyles she had slayed on me as a testimony of her craft. Getting a little aggravated with my unenthusiastic energy, Jacqui put the flat iron back in the stove and grabbed one of my photos from her station.

"Jan, here!" She said, placing a picture in front of me. "Send this one, Jan! You've got plenty of pictures to send, so find one– fill out the application online and go for it! Your gray hair will be a hit!"

Jacqui was so convincing that I started to sit up a little taller in her salon chair. My confidence was growing, and in my mind, I was beginning to see myself in New York City, hobnobbing with photographers and makeup artists on the set.

If I win, I would be representing so many overlooked women because of their age or gray hair. Then, the thought crossed my mind, *What if they insist on dyeing my gray hair? Nah. They wouldn't do that. Or would they?*

But as I quickly weighed the pros and cons, the pros definitely outweighed the cons. A free trip to New York City– my sons would be so proud of me. Heck, I would be so proud of me. And the cash prize wasn't bad either.

Jan, you can do this! I told myself with newfound confidence. *Being selected could be the opportunity of a lifetime. And even if I didn't win, at least I tried and represented older Black women and gray heads.*

That day, I promised Jacqui that I would send a photo, complete the submission form, and enter the competition. Jacqui believed in me and was so pleased.

And you know what? Jacqui was right!

In 2012, *MORE* magazine selected me out of more than 2,000 women across the country for an all-expenses-paid trip to New York City for a professional photo shoot and a feature in the magazine, and a $5,000 cash prize! All because of my youthfulness and gray hair. I was 55 years old. It was surreal.

But I didn't stop there. Three years later, at age 58, I won the *Essence* magazine Ageless Beauty contest, selected from hundreds of women in the 50–60 age category. Again, an all-expenses-paid trip to New York City. Another photo shoot with more recognition and visibility— an absolute dream.

Over the years, magazines featuring my photos, nationally and internationally, have brought not only blessings but also some burdens. While my image began to circulate widely in magazines, it was also used for marketing campaigns. Another nod to how your image can unfortunately be misused, not just for a fake dating profile.

On the internet, my photos have been widely circulated– often without my permission– for example, on Pinterest. I didn't put them there. And when I visit beauty salons, it's usually shared with me that the beauty industry "borrows" my image for advertisements. Again, the nerve.

But the most significant violation of using my photos is when wig companies use my pictures in magazine print ads. I mean, my hair is real. It's really *my* hair that I grew on *my* head. My hair is not synthetic, and my hair and I are *not* fake.

So, when friends showed me that the photos from the magazines I posed for were used in wig advertisements without my permission, another line had been crossed. This is theft. What has taken me years of courage to embrace– my real, natural gray, my identity, my story, and my life– is now suddenly being repurposed to sell someone else's idea of beauty. It bothers me not just because my image was taken, but because my truth was twisted. To see my photos used without my consent and reduced to a marketing tool is violating. It reminds me how easily women's bodies and choices are often treated as public property.

If you Google gray hair, Black women with gray hair, Black women with pixie cuts, older Black women with short hair, or gray pixie cuts, my photos often pop up. Before going viral on the internet, I had no idea my hair would get this much attention. Gray had been with me since I was a teenager. It felt normal to me– a part of life. But widespread media attention has a way of shifting your awareness– sometimes uncomfortably– especially your self-awareness.

Gray is Not for the Faint of Heart

Having gray hair can be uncomfortable. Gray hair doesn't let me hide. It's a conversation starter. It's an ice-breaker. For some reason, people feel comfortable asking me questions about my gray hair that lead to additional questions having nothing to do with it. I have firsthand experience with these questions, as some people think they can get all up in *my business,* asking the craziest questions. While some people ask well-meaning questions, others ask very inappropriate ones.

And when I say inappropriate, we're talking *inappropriate* to the max! Take, for example, the time a good girl friend's brother asked me, "Jan, are you gray all over– you know? In other places on your body, or just on your head?"

At that moment, I thought, *That's a very personal question for someone who hasn't earned an individual answer.* With a deadpan, wide-eyed look, I gave him the answer he needed, and not the one he wanted.

"Some things are gray, and some things are none of your business," I answered without cracking a smile.

His question wasn't about curiosity. It was about entitlement. And in that moment, I understood how quickly a woman's body can become open for commentary.

The Rumble at the Stadium

And of course, I can't forget the intrusiveness of random strangers attempting to touch my hair. That is a Black woman *no-no* that happens far too often, resulting in me having to say, "No, you cannot touch my hair." But one unsuspecting stranger had to learn that *no-no* the hard way.

Years ago, my ex-husband and I were attending an NCAA basketball game at the Palace of Auburn Hills in Michigan, and had suite tickets– great seats, mind you. The arena was sold out with deafening cheers from an overenthusiastic crowd.

However, while sitting in my seat enjoying the nail-biting game, I suddenly felt the unwanted cold and sweaty fingers of a hand caressing the back of my hair and scalp. Immediately, I jumped forward in my seat in shock, then looked behind me at a middle-aged, slightly balding White man with blue eyes wearing a Michigan State sports shirt.

"Hey, stop!" I yelled at the man. "What are you doing?" The crowd was so loud, and I felt I was fighting this battle alone because my husband was preoccupied with the game and not concerned with me at the time which was understandable.

Sitting down, I gathered myself and looked back at the man behind me and asked him, "Did you put your hands in my hair?" The man looked at me and said nothing– so I let it go. But I truly felt violated. But what happened next truly surprised me.

It was halftime, and that was the opportunity to go into our suite for drinks and food. I was ready for some refreshments, but as I was getting ready to enter the suite, my husband held me back and said, "I heard you say something to that man behind you. Did he put his hands in your hair?" I was stunned by his question because he was so engrossed in the second quarter of the game, I thought he didn't notice the stranger's infraction. I reluctantly responded "Yes" to him.

Oh boy! All hell broke loose.

In the suite, during halftime, my husband confronted the man about his action, and it wasn't a pretty sight. Let's just say the halftime show was not on the basketball court– but in our suite. Yes, this man had crossed a boundary, and it was totally inappropriate. He deserved the verbal beat-down he received.

So, yes, to this day, inappropriate and personal questions about my gray hair has led me and my family down some uncomfortable paths.

How Old Are You?

Another inappropriate and personal question revolves around age.

"Jan, how old are you?" is one question that often pops up wherever I go. I do understand that some people prefer not to share that information– and that's perfectly fine. It can be uncomfortable when your hair dominates the conversation, especially when you're around friends, family, or colleagues. Sometimes, I want to talk about anything other than my hair to simply exist without question and explanation. But visibility doesn't always give you that option, and curiosity rules the day. But as you can probably tell by now, I will tell anyone my age. I'm proud. I'm loud about it.

However, one of the quirks about being gray is that it can sometimes confuse people. Personally, first, they are trying to figure out *why* my hair is gray, and second, why I let it go gray, at whatever age they think I am. When you have gray hair, many people struggle to place you in the *age* category. Many see gray hair and think "old," but then they see a vibrant, confident woman who doesn't match the narrative they've been taught. This can really trip some people up.

It seems people want to know my age the way they want to know about the weather. The question is typically asked casually, constantly, and with a little side judgement. It pops up in conversations with strangers, friends of friends, and people who think curiosity is a free pass.

So, is it intrusive? At times.

But I've learned it's less about my age and gray hair and more about their need to place me somewhere on a timeline, in a box, or in a category that makes sense to them. Age, especially once your hair is gray, can feel like public property, as if the silver or white grants permission to ask what year you were born.

I don't think most people mean what they say with their questions. They're just curious.

Now, let me take you on a little stroll through my daily life when these questions emerge. So, many times when

I'm at a department store, the TSA checkpoint at the airport, or anywhere I need to show my ID, people will look at my photo, then look at my date of birth, then gaze at my gray hair, and that's when the questions begin.

"How long have you had gray hair?" "What color is that in your hair?" These questions go on and on. And those who don't ask, look at me in wonder, but I know they want to ask the gray hair questions. So, I let them wonder.

Be different.

Keep them guessing.

Shoulders back.

Stand tall.

Talk your talk.

And show them what you're working with.

The Oprah Effect

Here is my Oprah story. Yes. *Thee* Oprah.

Back in 2003, Oprah visited downtown Detroit as a special guest speaker at a fundraiser for *Perfecting Church* that drew over 2,000 people.

The health care system I worked for was a sponsor, and as the Chief Marketing Officer (CMO), I represented our system at the event, which included a VIP pre-event reception with only 150 guests. Being a HUGE Oprah fan, and I mean huge, I was honored and so excited to have this opportunity to meet Ms. Winfrey. My anticipation before the event was at an all-time high. I was nervous and thrilled all at the same time. So much so that I practiced for days what I was going to say to her if I had the chance to grace her presence at the private reception.

At that time, Oprah was sporting a bad-ass haircut. If I remember correctly, it was her chin-length bob flip. Well, that's how I would describe it. Anyway, I loved that hairstyle, so I decided that if I had the chance to have a brief chat with Ms. O, I would compliment her hair and, of course, tell her how much I admired her.

But guess what happened?

It went like this.

I'm in the receiving line waiting to greet Oprah.

She was two feet away. Yes, she was coming. The room was crowded and brimming with excitement! I was so nervous. My knees were shaking.

The receiving line moved slowly, and with every step closer to Oprah, the energy in the room thickened, like electricity before a summer storm. You could feel it. The conversations kept dropping to whispers and then dissolving into nervous laughter. Everyone stood a little straighter, adjusting their clothes a little more, and

I'm sure they rehearsed their one perfect sentence in their heads. I know I did.

By the time I could see her clearly, the air felt charged with gratitude, awe, and the wild hope that somehow, in a few brief seconds, she might look at each of us with something more than just another face passing by.

I rehearsed my compliment one more time. And then it was like the heavens opened up. And she appeared. *Hallelujah!*

Jan, don't mess this up! Oprah is here!

I reached out to shake Oprah's hand. She immediately grabbed my hand, and before I could get a word out, she smiled and said, "Oh my God! I love your hair! It's so beautiful on you. Your gray hair is beautiful!"

I looked at her, smiling but in shock, and said, "Thank you."

That's it. That's my Oprah story.

That moment taught me a valuable lesson. Sometimes, we underestimate what others see in us. We can be so critical and so hard on ourselves as are our own harshest critics, measuring ourselves by what we believe we lack rather than our positives. Sometimes, we zoom in on every flaw, while others see our strength, our light, our quiet resilience. It's strange how easily we can believe the worst about ourselves and how hard it is to accept the better version we see reflected in ourselves. Sometimes the people around us recognize our worth long before we do– and their faith becomes a mirror, reminding us of the beauty that has been out of focus, blurred, and too close to see.

I was not expecting a compliment from Oprah Winfrey. Not in a million years. But she saw something special in me, just like I saw something special in her.

This experience taught me more profound lessons as well. That being gray isn't about hair. It's about presence. And once you claim that, there is no going back.

CHAPTER SIX

Public Image Has Responsibilities

Since receiving so much attention for my hair, I have had to ask myself a deeper question: *What do I do with it?*

My gray hair has been good to me. It has opened doors, created opportunities, and introduced me to people and experiences I never imagined for myself. But more than that, it has inspired me to do things I never thought I could achieve. Essentially, my hair has given me courage.

Courage– really? I know what you're thinking. How can gray hair inspire courage?

Well, gray hair certainly teaches lessons. It teaches me to show up without a cover in a quiet but public way. To me, every gray hair is an act of defiance against a world that worships youthfulness and perfection. And everyone whom I have personally convinced not to cover their gray hair has needed a bit of courage. For many, it's a brave and bold move to rock gray hair. And for others, it's a scary process to make a physical change.

While gray hair may seem insignificant to some, to others, it is the crown of glory that mirrors original and authentic beauty.

Hair is often the first thing we notice about a person. When we change our hair, insecurity can set in, and we begin to ask self-doubting questions: *Will I look the same? Will I still be attractive? Will I be noticed for the right reasons? Or will I shrink into the crowd?*

My gray hair has trained me to be more confident, to stand out, to be okay with being seen, to be different, and to stand taller. Over time, what started as a physical change became an inner one with my hair shaping my courage, and my courage reshaping how I saw my hair.

Courage Demands Something in Return

My gray hair gave me a series of unexpected gifts. It gave me freedom from comparison, relief from constant maintenance, and permission to show up just as I am, as Jan. It gifted me visibility in a different way, not for youth or perfection, but for authenticity. The outward changes in my hair slowly revealed more profound truths about identity, aging, courage, and belonging. But *these* lessons have come over time.

Time and time again, my gray hair has revealed lessons I never expected to learn. So many, in fact, that I made a conscious decision to give back by sharing my experiences with others. My hair changed how I saw, treated, and perceived myself. For years, I tried to hold closely onto a previous version of Janice. But the real gift has been letting that change ripple outward, transforming from something personal into something publicly shared. So, giving back became a natural extension of who I am and my journey. To all sisters, I offer encouragement when women are in doubt, hope when they feel shame, and wisdom when they are struggling with transitioning to gray hair, drawing on my personal experiences. In some way, I am being the hero I have seen in others, such as Muhammad Ali.

Meeting My Hero

When I think of courage, my mind instantly goes to the life and legacy of my hero, Louisville-native Muhammad Ali. While he has many famous and highly recognized quotes, the most profound is, "Service to others is the rent you pay for your room here on earth." Ali repeated this statement many times in speeches and interviews, and believed deeply in helping people, lifting others, and using his social, political, and cultural influence for the good of humanity. As a global humanitarian and symbol of Black confidence and pride, Ali embodies courage. He stood firm in his beliefs, even when it cost him titles, money, and public approval. Watching Ali identify as a conscientious objector, which I am certain was uncomfortable, taught me many lessons with the most profound being that courage isn't about being fearless. It's about being faithful to who you are, even when it's unpopular.

In 1979, I had the opportunity to meet Ali. My late uncle, Rev. Charles Mims, who was a childhood friend of Ali, gave me passes to attend a reception honoring him in Louisville for his third heavyweight championship title, becoming the first fighter to do so. I was beyond excited. When I met the Champ, his presence wasn't GOAT-like, but rather angelic. I was mesmerized. There was a light shining all around him.

I was in awe. And yes, he was pretty, as he always joked about. But it was his *presence* that spoke volumes.

Years later, on June 10, 2016, with the passing of Muhammad Ali, I was yet again honored to join dignitaries and throngs of family and friends who gathered to say goodbye to the Greatest of All Time at a somber yet celebratory memorial service at an indoor arena in downtown Louisville, Kentucky.

Some of the speakers eulogizing Ali were Former President Bill Clinton, Billy Crystal, Bryant Gumbel, Oscar Award-winning actor Will Smith, Mike Tyson, Lennox Lewis served as pallbearers, and my brother–the Rev. Dr. Kevin Wayne Cosby, senior pastor at my home church, St. Stephen Church, and 13th President of Simmons College of Kentucky, the 107th and last designated Historically Black College and University (HBCU) in Louisville, Kentucky.

During the eulogy, my brother Kevin highlighted Ali's impact on Black self-love and dignity, framing him as a product of the civil rights struggle who "dared to love Black people." Although Ali was not physically present, his *presence* was felt throughout the Center.

My brother, Kevin, also talked about how Ali, during a time of self-doubt for Black people, boldly affirmed the beauty of Blackness, saying, "I'm Black!" and "I'm pretty!" which were considered oxymorons at the time.

So, what is the connection between my hero, Muhammad Ali, and my gray hair?

Actually– everything.

Both my gray hair and Ali taught me to stand in truth when the world expects you to hide.

While Ali showed me that courage is choosing yourself even when people disapprove, my gray hair has taught me the same lesson in a quieter, more personal way. In choosing not to color my hair, I have made a public decision to live honestly in a culture that tells women to stay young, quiet, and agreeable. And like Ali, I learned that bravery doesn't always roar. Sometimes, it simply just shows up.

The Sharing Begins

People ask me all the time how I keep it all together. Why are you so positive? Where does your energy come from at almost 70? What products do you use? How do you stay confident? How do you embrace aging without fear?

The truth is that aging can be frightening. However, in actuality, we all are aging every single day, whether we acknowledge it or not. And for a long time, I answered those questions privately– one-on-one, in intimate conversations with women who reached out to me quietly. First, it began with family members and friends. And then it grew to some of my young employees and colleagues. During my professional career, I met so many women who asked me to be their mentor. Being in their presence reminds me of who I once was, and who I still am when I choose courage over caution.

For over 35 years, I've mentored young women of color and helped to launch their professional careers. There is something sacred about the exchange between generations of women. I offer them perspective, and they offer me renewal. And most importantly, their questions keep me honest.

Mentoring is also sharing beauty secrets and suggestions with anyone who asks. Oftentimes, when I'm at a party, the grocery store, the gym, or airport, I'm asked, "How do you keep your gray hair so silver and white?" If I had a dime for every time someone has asked me that question, I would be a wealthy woman. I am open about my hair journey, my life's ups and downs, the good and the bad. And sharing my journey with others is one of the ways I choose to give back to my community. Muhammad Ali used his platform to lift others. My gray hair gave me my platform to not lift myself, but other women around me.

The Detour

On a cold January day, I received a three-way call from my sisters, which is something we often do– chat for hours. My sister Natalie told me that I often came up in conversations with her girl friends because they couldn't believe my age and wanted to know my beauty secrets to look young. Nat would tell them that her big sis, "Jan was a UNICORN, a one of a kind when it came to aging."

But this call was different. Natalie, my youngest sister, was matter-of-fact and stepped in as if she were THE older sister. Sylvia, who often plays the role of good cop– she's an attorney– took on a vocal role in Natalie's "Amen" corner.

Nat said that I needed to get my act together, start a podcast, and stop procrastinating. "Jan, you've got something to offer so many people, so let's go. Just do it!" said my Nat with Sylvia chiming in agreement.

"I ordered you a ring light so you can start creating videos," continued Natalie.

Right then and there, I made a promise to my sisters that I would give it a try, but in the back of my mind, I was still unsure.

A few days later, a large box arrived at my front door. Puzzled, I scanned the box over, trying to remember what I had ordered online that week. The box wasn't heavy. However, it had been raining that day, so the bottom was a little wet and challenging to get a good grip on to lift. Grabbing the wet box on both sides, I awkwardly carried the package through my front door, still trying to figure out what I had ordered. But when I finally opened the box, I just stood there.

I was in shock. *Dang it, Natalie. You were really serious about this.* But I wasn't ready for prime time! Not yet.

It was a ring light. The same ring light that Natalie told me she would send.

Natalie is really serious about me going public and not hiding under a bushel, I remember thinking.

This called for an immediate phone call to Nat. I thanked her for the gift, then asked her the only question on my mind.

"What the hell am I supposed to do now?"

Laughing, she calmly said, "Jan, just talk. Speak from your heart. Talk about the things that matter to you. I'm confident it will resonate with others."

Nat made it sound so simple. But it wasn't that simple for me. For over 35 years, I worked in healthcare marketing, communications, and public relations. I was good at it– really good. But my role was always behind the scenes. I promoted organizations, causes, and other people. I spoke on behalf of something. Now, I had to talk about myself. And that was uncomfortable, especially going live on social media. I felt exposed. Vulnerable. Awkward. I worried about how I would sound, how I would look. Whether anyone would even care. But eventually, I realized something important.

I had something to offer.

I had something to give.

And then I thought– for over 35 years, I had mentored women privately whom I affectionately refer to as my "youngins," and I have also mentored my younger sisters and girl friends. Sharing advice and listening, encouraging, and being honest about aging, confidence, beauty, careers, relationships, and life.

So, why not reach a wider audience? I asked myself this question for about six months.

Well, finally, on June 27, 2025, *Jan's Gray Glam* was born.

What started as a weekly Facebook video series became a space for real conversations. Honest ones. Unfiltered ones. Dialogue about make-up products, exercise, menopause, fashion, wrinkles, dry skin, confidence, reinvention, and self-worth. The women who have listened to or contributed to the conversations have shared their inspiration with me. But I, too, have been inspired by these conversations because what I have discovered is that many of us go through the same things, have the same questions, insecurities, and hopes. And this realization has taught me many lessons, with the primary one being to live out loud.

Should I wear this?

Is it too late to try that?

Am I still desirable?

Am I enough?

This "living out loud" phase of my life is the most significant one yet– not because of attention, but because of purpose and because it means I no longer soften my truth to make other people comfortable. And I no longer hide the part of myself that once felt visible or vulnerable. This phase has reshaped how I move through the world. I speak more clearly, love more boldly, and trust myself more deeply.

My mission as a gray-haired woman has allowed me to give back in rewarding ways. It's like I am high on living– on life itself– and the possibilities that still exist. I cannot overstate this enough.

Women of all ages need a voice. We need to be seen and heard. And my mission is to do just that.

All Women Must Use Their Voice

Every woman carries a voice inside her, but not every woman learns to use her voice. From an early age, many of us learn to soften our opinions, swallow our anger, and shrink ourselves so that others can feel more comfortable. Too often, we are praised for our agreeableness, quietness, and friendliness. Meanwhile, our boldness is labeled "troubled" and "bitchy." Over time, that can make a woman doubt her own thoughts, beliefs, and ultimately, herself, leading to silence.

I know I've personally struggled to be both seen and heard in many spaces, including boardrooms, classrooms, workplaces, and even in relationships. And when we emote, we are dismissed as being overreactive. Our voice is criticized, no matter the decibel level. These judgments can be exhausting. And while my voice is a gift, I didn't always see it that way.

Finding My Voice and My Passion

There was a time when I didn't have a voice, didn't know what I was going to do with my life, and thought I had nothing to contribute. Nothing to offer. I was a pastor's wife, and kind of lost. I was uncertain about my education and career path. It wasn't black or white and took several turns, where I ended up on a road less traveled. Not the wrong road, nor the right one either. But a gray road. See, I was taught early on to rush towards a decision, choose a career path, define myself, and get that degree and a job. So, inevitably, my growth happened in the gray. However, that all changed when I went back to school to finish my college degree as an adult and reclaimed my voice– my most precious gift.

Born and raised in Louisville, Kentucky, I graduated from Ballard High School in 1974. During my college career, my education and career path took several turns. I began as a music major at Knoxville College, which is no longer in operation, in Knoxville, Tennessee. Shortly afterwards, I changed my focus to public relations at Wayne State University in Detroit, Michigan. Between those two majors was a 16-year gap. In other words, I earned my degree 16 years after graduating from high school. That occurred for a variety of reasons: I got married, became a pastor's wife, moved to Detroit, and had two sons– and a lot more in between.

When I graduated from Wayne State University in 1990, I knew that I was smart, intelligent, and a good writer. I loved school and learning. I was a sponge. And my GPA was through the roof. I even received a tuition-based scholarship, paying my way through college.

But I felt I didn't have a voice. And as I continued my college trajectory, I wasn't sure about my major. However, I was still leaning towards journalism. In this career field, my voice could be amplified on media platforms on local, national, and international levels.

Since most of my college classes were in communications, I spent most of my time in Manoogian Hall. I loved being in that building. It felt like a key to my future, where every student and teacher were on the same page. Even now, when I think about it, Manoogian Hall felt like a home. But I must admit that I was also very uncomfortable because I was "the older student" with gray hair. And yes, I stood out, not because of my gray hair, but because I didn't associate with other students, was only concerned about getting straight As, and getting home to my sons at night.

As a Communications major and like all students in the program, I was assigned a counselor– Dr. James Measell– Department Chair of the Public Relations (PR) Department. Dr. Measell was an outspoken, thin, White man with dark hair and glasses who dressed conservatively, usually wearing a pullover sweater and tie. He was an excellent counselor and teacher.

During our first meeting, Dr. Measell asked me, "Janice, what major have you selected?"

"I'm still unsure," I said. "But I think it will be Communications/Journalism."

Dr. Measell, then, responded, "Okay, that's fine, but I think you would be a really strong Public Relations major. Do you know anything about Public Relations?"

I had no clue.

So, Dr. Measell went on to explain more and gave me some printed info about the PR department. I told him I would review it and get back with him the following week.

After reading the materials and doing a little research, I made the life-changing decision to become a Public Relations major. Dr. Measell was pleased, and he became my most prominent advocate, supporter, and cheerleader. Finally, my voice was heard, appreciated, and loud.

Yes, I indeed found my voice and my passion. However, I found it at an older age. Yes, the ripe age of 34. And there's nothing wrong with that! I was married with two young sons by the time I finished my degree and began my career in marketing and public relations. I know you've heard it over and over again that it's never too late, but it's the truth. It wasn't too late for me, a middle aged gray head to find my way. To start fresh. To begin again. And to have a tremendous impact. My gray hair didn't stop me and my age didn't stop me either.

CHAPTER SEVEN

The Myth of Aging Alone

While we all age, we do not age alone. The same thing that is happening to us physically during the aging process– the changes in our bodies– is happening to every person around us. Aging is not an isolated event or journey. Aging links all of us to generations of people who have come before us and those who will follow us. I believe if we see aging this way, we will not age alone.

I have girl friends who are caring for their aging parents, and my friends sometimes forget that they are aging too. I also have young mentees who are in the prime of their careers, in wonderful marriages, have dutiful husbands and amazing kids, and they forget that they are aging. We are an "aging community." Growing together, living together, learning together, and aging together. As members of an aging community, we can encourage and learn from one another's victories, if we choose to tap into the voices who shaped us, such as our mothers, grandmothers, aunts, sisters, and mentors, and people we have watched from afar.

My life has been nothing short of fascinating. As mentioned in an earlier chapter, my mother died at the young age of 36 when I was just 12 years old and left four beautiful children. However, what I didn't mention is that one year after my mom passed away, my dad remarried a lovely woman named Connie, whom we lovingly call CC.

CC is a real character. She is loving, extremely smart, funny, opinionated, audacious, very well read, a world traveler, loves art, and yes– she's a gray head. Connie is a bit of a revolutionary. To give you a clue– she was at the March on Washington on August 28, 1963, when she was a teenager. Let me put it this way– CC was ahead of her time. And she raised her children– and loved us– to do the same, while teaching the power of authenticity, independence, and courage.

Growing up in Louisville, Kentucky, CC encouraged my siblings and me to experience the world beyond what we could see right in front of us. She believed travel mattered. Exposure mattered. Curiosity mattered. And her encouragement pushed us to be bold and to take risks– even when it felt uncomfortable.

When I think about my early influences, it was CC who had the most significant impact, emphasizing the importance of sisterhood and giving back. In a world where women are too often pitted against one another, CC taught me that women don't just survive but carry one another.

As previously shared, I have a little sister with a beautiful head of salt-and-pepper hair in her own right, and I have another amazing, beautiful younger sister, Sylvia– also a proud gray head. The three of us are like a little tribe. And when we're together, it's a hoot. And if you add CC to the mix, it's a family sit-com with all the dysfunctionality included!

No– I genuinely mean it. It's loud. It's chaotic. It's laughter layered with honesty. It's crazy in the best possible way.

These three women– CC, Natalie, and Sylvia– are critical to my life. They inspire me constantly. They lift me when I'm tired. They support me when I'm unsure. They are the bedrock of my foundation outside of my husband, Dean, and my sons.

These three women have taught me how to be selfless; how to look inward; and, most importantly; how to be my most authentic self.

I do not need my sisters to be less, for me to feel like more. This sisterhood I share with my "sisters" is a sacred bond, not defined by blood or family ties. The same connection can develop for all women when we choose connection over competition and support over judgment. I've learned that sisterhood is encouragement spoken honestly, but lovingly, and celebrating one another without envy.

My Youngins

Sisterhood has always been a central part of my life, and it started within my family unit. But over time, it expanded far beyond blood and extended into the community.

Throughout my marketing career, I have had the privilege of meeting– and mentoring– some truly remarkable young women. I've mentioned them before and call them my "youngins." These women inspire me just as much as I hope I inspire them. In many ways, they've kept me young, and I desperately need these women in my life. Being around them means I stay informed on everything from new slang I barely understand to fashion trends I swore I would never wear—until somehow *I do.* Their confidence, boldness, and unapologetic self-expression constantly remind me that womanhood is always evolving. They ask questions many of us are too afraid to ask. They walk into rooms already believing they belong there. And while I may offer them wisdom about patience, grace, and surviving life's hard seasons, they return the favor by teaching me flexibility, laughter, and how not to take myself too seriously.

Womanhood— I've realized— includes many traits: resilience, nurturing, intuition, strength, style, humor, and the ability to reinvent yourself at any age. The truth is, mentoring them doesn't drain me— it energizes me. Somewhere between giving advice and laughing at their stories, I realize I am helping raise future generations of beautiful women. But there's a great trade-off. They come to me for wisdom, and I go to them to make sure I'm *still culturally relevant.*

My "youngins" keep me laughing. I usually meet with them one-on-one— for brunch, lunch, or dinner. They share their fears, dreams, and career goals. They challenge me. They guide me through new, uncharted waters. In return, I'm available to them– to talk honestly about complex subjects, relationships, aging, confidence, and life in general.

Rosie Reebel, a beautiful and brilliant young woman, was one of my first mentees and youngin. Rosie was my intern while I was Director of Communications at Sinai Grace Hospital in Detroit, Michigan. She was so eager to learn, and Rosie excelled at every level, even while sitting at the crowded corner at my desk in my small office on the executive wing of the corporate office. I knew it was uncomfortable for Rosie, but she didn't seem to mind. Because of our proximity every day, Rosie was privy to every work meeting, discussion, project plan, future event, and happenings in my private life. Rosie and I developed a special bond without even trying. It just evolved. And it evolved into something beautiful.

When Rosie got engaged, I felt like her second mom! I was so proud of her, and I couldn't wait for the wedding day. Unfortunately, I was unable to attend the ceremony because I was relocating to Indianapolis. But Rosie made an unusual request of me regarding the preparations of her special day. Even to this day, thinking about her request gives me goosebumps.

"Jan, I know you can't make it to the wedding," explained Rosie, but I would be honored if you would design and make my wedding veil."

I couldn't believe she remembered I could sew! Of course, I told her yes. And although I didn't attend the ceremony in person, I couldn't help but feel a special connection to Rosie that day— hundreds of miles away.

And yes, I share all my beauty secrets with my youngins. I owe them that.

Another youngin of mine wanted a complete makeover, and asked me to go with her to the mall to make it happen. Trying on different clothes in various styles and getting a makeover at the MAC counter was so much fun. We even took a trip to the ophthalmologist to exchange her eyeglasses for contacts. Talk about a *transformation!* But the most satisfying part of the experience was watching my youngin evolving into a *grown-ass* woman. Her confidence grew exponentially that day.

What I've learned over the years is life is not about hoarding knowledge or gatekeeping everything for yourself. It's about opening the door for others. It's about helping prepare others to thrive once they step through the door. When Rosie finished her internship with me, I recommended her for her first job at a small Public Relations firm owned by a friend of mine. And then, I recommended Rosie for her next job. And then her next. And today Rosie is a successful Director of Marketing Strategy and Insights for a prominent health system in Palo Alto, California. I'm a proud *mama!*

I've offered paid and unpaid internships– because experience counts too– to so many young women *and* young men. I've met with so many young professionals, one-on-one, to give them career advice and the opportunity to shadow me on the job. And I've hired many who had little or no work experience also. Someone did that for me.

In 1990, two months after I graduated from college, Janice Simmons, a beautiful Black woman and Vice President of Marketing and Communications, hired me for my first healthcare position at Pontiac General Hospital in Pontiac, Michigan. During my last interview for the position, Janice told me I was one of the three final candidates and honestly confided that I was the least qualified because I had just graduated and had *no* experience. But she told me, "Jan, if you promise me that you will do your best, learn all you can, I'm going to hire you and give you the opportunity." I promised her I would do my best— and Janice Simmons opened the door to my career in healthcare marketing when I was just a youngin.

And I am eternally grateful.

See, sisterhood, isn't always about blood or proximity. It's also about intention.

There are many women I admire deeply whom I don't know personally. Mothers, Teachers, Ministers, Nurses, Physicians, Executives, and many others who don't know me, but who have inspired me from afar. And there are women I have gone out of my way to meet because they unknowingly touched my life in some way.

When I first moved to Detroit many years ago, I watched– at a distance– a beautiful, brilliant gray-haired woman. She was an executive, and when she spoke, people listened. Every time I was in her presence, I was always mesmerized by every word she said. Not to mention, her gray haircut was always on point. She was impossible to overlook— not just because of her hair, but because she was the first woman of any race or ethnicity who I had seen in a leadership position wearing her gray hair so confidently. A beautiful Black woman, somewhere in her fifties, it seemed her gray hair was so natural for her— like her signature. Her silver strands cast a soft light on her face, highlighting her radiant skin. Her gray hair wasn't dull or fading—it shimmered a beautiful blend of silver, pearl, and soft tones. There was wisdom in her eyes, grace in her posture, and a calmness that made me look twice. Her beauty wasn't chasing youth. And her gray did not age her— it refined her. *True elegance.*

As I watched her over the years, I realized I wanted to be just like that woman. Not simply because she was beautiful and stylish, but because she seemed so completely at ease with herself. She wore her gray hair with confidence. And I hoped that one day I would carry myself with the same confidence and comfort.

Eventually, I had the opportunity to meet her, Vernice Anthony. Although we never worked together, we occasionally would cross paths, always with warmth and mutual regard. Our connection was not rooted in friendship, but in quiet admiration. And to this day, every time I see her, I remind her how much she meant to a young executive like me.

I stand on her shoulders.

And I hope that I'm doing for someone else what Vernice did for me– especially when I don't even realize someone is watching.

I want to be that beacon of hope and quiet proof that if a gray-haired woman like me can thrive, lead, love, and live fully, then so can other women.

Because the truth is simple: we do not age alone.

CHAPTER EIGHT

Redefining Beauty, Age, and Power

When and why did aging become something women were expected to apologize for?

At age 18, I was aging. At age 40, I was aging. If you are reading or listening to this book, you, too, are aging. Minute by minute. Hour by hour. Second by second. Both women and men. We can't stop it. So, why are the natural progression and physical signs of aging, like graying hair, treated as a negative? For many of us, becoming a gray head is inevitable.

As a little girl, my hair was aging, and for so long, people treated my gray hair as something different, odd, or a flaw that needed to be covered and corrected.

I don't know when or why we started associating graying and aging with something other than beauty. But it seems that women of all ages have faced the same perplexing decisions about aging for centuries.

Should I buy into the stereotypes and do everything in my power and pocketbook to correct or reverse the aging process? Or do I go in, full throttle, and embrace the inevitable? There is so much social pressure to "look young," which can create unnecessary stress in our everyday lives. From media images, workplace expectations, and casual comments from friends or strangers, the message is often subtle but constant– *stay young and look fresh.* That pressure can turn regular natural changes– such as graying– into sources of anxiety. Pressure can influence how we style our hair, how we show up for work, how we date, and how we exist in our own skin. The emotional weight of constantly monitoring how we look can be exhausting. And the constant pressure we put on ourselves, or allow others to put on us, can unfortunately negatively affect our self-esteem, and even our mental health.

One day, while living in Indianapolis, Indiana, I went to Saks Fifth Avenue to just browse– not looking for anything in particular. Eventually, I found myself in the Women's shoe department, and as I browsed, I noticed a beautiful Black woman behind the service counter. I'm terrible at guessing someone's age, but I'd say she was about 65. She had a gorgeous face– coffee colored skin, taller than me, at about 5'8" with beautiful white teeth, and a long neck like supermodel Naomi Campbell. And she was dressed to the nines! Customers were keeping her very busy, but she was polite to everyone who approached her.

Since I happened to be in the department, I had to try on a few pairs of shoes. Just a few. When it was my turn to try on shoes, I told her I was in no hurry and that she could attend to the other customers before getting to me. By the time she finally got to me, there were very few customers in the department. Although this beautiful woman was accommodating, I noticed that when I asked her a question, she looked down, wouldn't make eye contact, and spoke rather quietly.

After leaving for a few minutes to bring out shoes for me to try on, including a pair of boots, she returned and quietly asked me how long I had been gray. I briefly shared my hair story during which she seemed intrigued by my gray hair and wanted to hear more. As I talked about my hair, for some reason, she immediately reminded me of my Aunt Betty because of her fair skin and very dark hair. This made me feel at ease with her as she lingered around me, picking up the many pairs of tried-on shoes scattered across the carpet. I could tell she was comfortable speaking with me too to the point that she mentioned that she had a break coming up and would love to treat me to a cup of coffee.

"I would really like to hear more about how you style and keep your gray hair so white," she said kindly. She seemed harmless and I felt safe, so I accepted her invitation.

"Sure, I would love to join you," I responded. "However, I don't drink coffee."

Laughing, she said, "Ok, I'll treat you to a hot herbal tea."

I chuckled, "You've got a date," I said, and waited patiently for 15 minutes while she cashed out two customers, then, walked into the back storage room while balancing six or seven shoe boxes cradled in her arms. I admit that her curiosity about my hair piqued my curiosity about her.

When my newfound friend walked back towards me, she smiled, and asked, ”How much time do you have?”

I winked and said, “I’ve got all the time in the world.”

We, then, walked to a small cafe sitting in the mall near Saks. When we sat down, I ordered my tea. She ordered a large cup of coffee. And that’s when she told me– a stranger– her story, and it was a very interesting one.

I’ll call her Mrs. Smith, for the sake of this book. Mrs. Smith was 70 years old. She shared that she was born and raised in Indianapolis, was married, and had adult children and grandchildren. Then the real questions began that I could tell she couldn’t wait to ask.

“How long have you been gray and how does your husband feel about it?”

“He loves it and, quite frankly, would be upset if I colored it,” I responded.

Now, sidenote, what I haven’t mentioned about Mrs. Smith yet is that her hair was a VERY, VERY dark black. It was so dark that it looked unusual. You could tell she dyed it often, and I could clearly see a little bit of gray peaking at her roots. So, what she was about to tell me made sense to what I had briefly observed.

Mrs. Smith shared that she had colored her hair for years because her husband felt she was unattractive with gray hair. She said prior to her then husband, she was gray for years and loved it, but then when she married her new husband, he wanted her to change her hair. She gave in and colored her hair, but prayed that he would be okay with her going back to having gray hair.

As she told me her hair story, she showed me photos of herself with a full head of gray hair. Can I tell you, and I'm not exaggerating– this woman looked gorgeous!!! OMG! She was beautiful and born to be a gray head.

She said she was so sad that she couldn't be her authentic self and didn't understand why her husband felt she was unattractive with gray hair. Her friends and family told her she looked younger, vibrant, and so attractive with her gray hair, and they didn't understand why she gave in to her new husband's beauty standards. But most importantly, she said that since she started coloring the gray, she hadn't felt quite like herself. Every time she looked in the mirror, she said she saw an imposter, which negatively affected how she viewed herself.

Her story made me incredibly sad and heartbroken for her. And although I had just met Mrs. Smith, I wanted so much more for her.

As we ended our conversation, I tried to offer an encouraging word. First, I wanted to acknowledge that her desire and need to look and feel a certain way were okay and valid.

"The photos you showed me of you with gray hair are beautiful," I told Mrs. Smith. "You are not wrong for wanting to stop dyeing your hair. The desire to live in alignment with who you authentically are is not a rebellion– although your husband may see it that way. It is a matter of self-respect. Hair might be a small thing, but to me it's a very personal thing and represents a big part of who you are. Your feelings do matter, and living every day in something that seems like a costume will eventually create resentment towards your husband."

I, then, encouraged her to have a calm, grounded conversation with her husband and to say something like, "I love you, and I hear that you prefer my hair dyed, but I don't feel like myself anymore when I dye it. I need you to support me in feeling comfortable and confident in my own body."

While giving Mrs. Smith my suggested "husband" script, I could tell she was getting emotional, her eyes filling with tears and glazing over. At that moment, I decided to switch gears and said, "And by the way, if you need a fabulous hair stylist who can have you rocking a bad-ass gray hair style, I've got the person for you! You definitely need a fly haircut!!!"

She laughed out loud as she fought back tears. I wrote down my stylist's number on a napkin and gave it to her. She graciously accepted it. I have no idea if Mrs. Smith had that conversation with her husband. But if she did, I hope her husband eventually saw and embraced the true beauty within his wife.

Who decided youth was the only version of beauty worth celebrating? Mrs. Smith's gray hair photos were a vision of beauty, and it made me wonder: *Who created the rulebook of beauty standards?*

Friendships in the Gray

I have two beautiful BFFs, Kristi and Carla. These ladies have been my ride or die for many years.

When I met Kristi in 2001, I was struck by her beauty. At the time, she had beautifully colored brown hair, and it was very becoming on her. But Kristi, who is 10 years younger than I am, became more comfortable letting her gray hair shine through. I never had a discussion with Kristi about becoming a gray head, and she wears it proudly today. And her hair is beautiful, just like her spirit.

But let me tell you about BFF Carla. I adore her. She is tall, has an immediate presence, is funny and incredibly giving, very stylish, looks younger than her age, and is drop-dead gorgeous.

When I met Carla in 2003, she was coloring her hair black to cover the gray that was coming in. She had enviable, thick hair with a cute cut she maintained religiously. However, I could see that Carla was covering her gray. We had a few conversations about it, and I tried to encourage her to go gray. I knew it would look incredible on her, but Carla said, "No way," and kept coloring her hair.

Many times, when Carla and I would have our GF meet-ups, I would get compliments from random people about my hair. The compliments would come so often that it became a running joke between Carla and me. So, when a compliment came my way in front of her, Carla would say, "OMG, I am so tired of hearing about your hair!" And the person giving the compliment would be taken aback, and then Carla would start laughing and say, "I'm just kidding." It was so funny, and we laughed about it for years.

I brought Carla up because I knew that Carla would be beautiful with gray hair, and I was hoping and praying that one day she would take the plunge. Carla and her husband moved from Michigan to Florida, so I didn't get to see my BFF as often. I deeply missed my friend. So, I was elated when Carla called to tell me she was coming to Detroit for a visit. We planned to meet at our favorite spot– Beverly Hills Grill. I couldn't wait to see her.

I was running late, but as soon as I arrived, Carla was already seated and in our favorite booth. I hugged my dear friend, we exchanged greetings, and we held on to one another as if we hadn't seen each other in years. But what happened next had me in tears.

When we finally sat down, and I looked at my friend, I was astonished! Sitting before me was my Carla, who had been coloring her hair for years, now with salt-and-pepper hair! She was absolutely BEAUTIFUL!! I was so emotional about it. *Did I overreact?* Probably. It's just hair, right? Carla was always beautiful, but at that moment, she was glowing. She was radiant. I mean, could she get even more beautiful?! Apparently, yes! Her shiny silver hair sparkled through, and I was mesmerized. She lit up the room.

I couldn't help but ask, "What made you decide to stop coloring your hair?" Carla's answer was simple.

"It was time," she said.

And that's all I needed to hear.

I could tell that Carla was serious and wasn't going to dye her hair again. Carla is a powerful woman, and once she has made up her mind, she is totally committed. But there was something different about her attitude. It was as if she stepped fully into herself–no filters, no apologies. She didn't elaborate on "her why," and I didn't ask her to explain further. Carla didn't need to make a dramatic announcement about it. It was a quiet announcement. No fanfare. But it was clear to me that I was witnessing what courage truly looks like. Carla chose truth over approval, and seeing that kind of courage is unforgettable because it gives the rest of us permission to step into our whole selves.

Today, Carla's hair is almost entirely gray. And you know what? She's stopped all the time about her hair, and I swear she looks 15 years younger. Carla is a walking testimony that gray hair doesn't age you. It reveals you.

Unrealistic American Beauty Standards

Historically, in American culture, wrinkles have been framed as flaws. It's unfortunately true. Gray hair is treated like a problem to be solved. Getting older is positioned as something to fight, hide, or delay as long as possible. And beauty is seen as rigid, standardized, and narrowly defined, and handed to us quietly and repeatedly– through advertising, entertainment, workplace expectations, and even well-meaning advice.

Dye your hair. Dress younger. Don't let yourself go. Fix this. Smooth that. Correct everything – as if aging equates to failure.

If you are over 40, society seems to say that you can't be authentically beautiful in America. To be attractive in America has meant fitting a narrowly defined aesthetic. Beauty is symmetry, facial-feature balance, smooth skin, thinness, certain hair textures, and features closest to Eurocentric norms.

But who made those social norms and beauty standards?

As women, we are so critical of ourselves that it's hard for us to look in the mirror and say the words, "I'm beautiful." Not to mention all the online editing features used to filter how we look to fit American beauty standards.

But I actively challenge those standards. Women every day are redefining beauty as authenticity rather than perfection. We are seeing more natural hair, textured hair, diverse body types, aging skin, disability representation, and women on social media are showing flaws and all. As women, *we* need to decide what beautiful means, rather than leave it to culture, the beauty industry, or trends. Let's give beauty a new look and a new attitude. My gorgeous friend, Ketly Williams, wears her beautiful bald head with grace and challenges everything we've been taught about what beauty is supposed to look like. And while we are at it, let's give gray hair a new attitude. As a gray head- I'm loud and proud! Instead of waiting for permission to be seen and accepted by the masses, let's disrupt the narrative.

Gray hair disrupts that narrative. Gray hair on a woman challenges the idea that power fades with time. It exposes the lie that relevance has an expiration date. Power and beauty do not dissipate with age– but deepen. And gray hair no longer needs to prove itself. Gray hair knows who it is.

A woman who has lived, loved, lost, and survived carries a presence that cannot be manufactured. No serum can replace it. No filter can replicate it.

And yet, we rarely see that version of beauty reflected to us.

Instead, women are encouraged to chase an earlier version of themselves– as if becoming who we are now is something to mourn. We are taught to preserve youth rather than honor growth. We want the lines around our eyes erased, the gray covered, and maturity, for some, translates as decline.

I reject that for myself. And I reject that for all women, including Mrs. Smith.

I reject the idea that growing older means becoming invisible. I reject the notion that confidence should soften, ambition should shrink, or beauty should have a deadline.

Gray hair didn't make me powerful. But it did reveal the power I already had.

It forced me to stand fully in who I am– without apology and without disguise. And in doing so, it reminded me that beauty isn't about being pleasing.

It's about being present.

And that brings me to something else we are rarely allowed to say out loud.

So, let me be blunt.

I'm 69.

And I am sexy.

Is that arrogant?

No. It's a fact– because it's how I feel and who I am.

I don't bow to textbook definitions or social media norms about what sexiness is supposed to look like. I don't subscribe to the idea that desire has an expiration date or that confidence should fade quietly with age.

Desire does not expire.

If you are sexy at 45, your sexiness is not put on a shelf at 75. It doesn't disappear just because society feels more comfortable pretending it does.

Yes, I am wise. But sensuality still exudes from my body, mind, and spirit.

Sexy isn't about tight skin or chasing youth. It's about ease. It's about comfort in your own skin. It's about confidence without performance. A woman who knows who she is and no longer needs permission carries a quiet magnetism that cannot be taught or duplicated. That kind of sexy doesn't fade with age.

It deepens.

When women stop competing with time, something remarkable happens. We reclaim ourselves– our worth. And we stop investing in the mundane *'I-have-to-please-everyone'* syndrome.

Ladies, this is your world.

This is your time.

This is your space.

There are no limitations– except the ones we accept.

You've just got to embrace who you are.

Own it.

And learn to be comfortable in your own skin.

That’s not arrogance– that’s power.

And I pray that Mrs. Smith, wherever she may be, found her power and embraced it.

Because it was always there.

CHAPTER NINE

What I Want Women to Know

So, I am sitting right here with you, telling you just one thing:

You are not late.

Not late to love.

Not late to purpose.

Not late to joy.

Not late to become who you are meant to be.

Many women walk around carrying an invisible clock, convinced they've missed their moment. That if something didn't happen by a certain age, the window has closed. I don't believe that, not for one second.

What I know now, and what I wish I had understood earlier, is that becoming is not something you age out of, but it's something you grow into.

There is one disheartening line I hear women 50 and above say over and over again, and it's the "I used to" line…

I used to do this. I used to do that.

I used to do that, but now that I'm older, I've stopped.

I used to exercise.

I used to eat healthy.

I used to wear makeup.

I used to care about my appearance.

I used to get my hair done.

I used to try new hairstyles.

I used to dress with intention.

I used to travel.

I used to believe in finding love again.

Every time I hear "*I used to…*" my heart sinks a little. And we blame it all on aging. Yes, there are some things that we cannot continue to do as we age for myriad reasons. But I hear many women cutting themselves off from possibilities that are still exciting and available to them.

Aging should not mean shutting down parts of yourself. It should not mean giving up curiosity, creativity, or self-expression. We should never stop evolving. We should never stop experimenting, learning, or trying new versions of ourselves.

Reinvention doesn't belong only to the young. If anything, aging gives us more permission to explore who we are and how we want to show up in the world.

I want to share something that perfectly illustrates my point.

I've mentioned my little sister Natalie throughout this book. Well, Natalie is preparing to get married for the very first time at the age of 53, and I am beyond excited for her.

But that is not the whole story.

Over the past few years, Natalie has completely changed her way of life.

She is healthier than she has ever been.

She's more confident.

She has lost over 50 pounds, added muscle to her frame, developed better eating habits, and carries herself with undeniable confidence.

She's rocking a fly new salt-and-pepper haircut.

She moved to a different city.

She dresses like a supermodel.

She walks with an "I am here to slay" attitude– and I absolutely love it.

And Natalie is happy!

What inspires me the most isn't just how Natalie looks, but who she has become.

She didn't wait for permission. She didn't decide it was too late. She didn't settle into who she used to be.

She chose growth. But it did reveal the power she already had. Change is always possible.

Watching my sister step fully into herself at this stage of her life has been a powerful reminder and testimony that change is always possible. Becoming the best version of yourself has no deadline.

But you have to make the decision to change. And that decision can happen at 30, at 50, at 70, or at any moment you decide you're ready.

Here is what I want women to know:

Confidence isn't about being loud. It doesn't announce itself. It settles in quietly once you stop asking for permission, once you stop explaining yourself, and when you realize you don't owe the world constant justification about who you are.

It is okay to change your mind. About people, your paths, and about what you thought you wanted. Growth will do that to you. And it doesn't mean you failed. It just means you listened to you!

Comparison will steal your joy faster than almost anything else. There will always be someone doing more, doing it differently, doing it louder. None of that diminishes your path. Your journey is not a competition.

Aging is not something to fear, but something to honor. I've personally learned to honor the aging process. And maybe that's why I celebrate my age out loud because life gets more comfortable, interesting, and powerful the older you get.

Being seen matters. Not for applause. Not for validation. But because your presence gives other women permission to be fully themselves.

And finally, there is no one way to age.

There is no one way to be powerful.

There is no one way to be beautiful.

But there is one requirement:

You have to show up– as you are.

CHAPTER TEN

A Gray-Fully Lived Life

There is *ONE* thing more than anything else, I hope you understand. This was *NEVER* just a book about hair.

Gray hair may have been the invitation to this book, but the real conversation has always been about permission. Permission to live fully, to age honestly, and to show up as yourself without apology. And believe me, it has taken me a long time to get here. I still have self-doubt at times. But when that doubt rears its ugly head, I do my best to tune it out, focus on a future of beautiful possibilities, and allow myself to grow in grace.

Growing older has taught me that grace is not about perfection. It's about acceptance. It's about understanding who you are, where you've been, and what truly matters now.

A gray-fully lived life is not one without mistakes. It's one where mistakes become teachers, not anchors holding you down. It's a life where you stop chasing who you used to be and start honoring who you are becoming.

I've learned that aging doesn't require reinvention every season– but it does require honesty.

Honest conversations.

Honest relationships.

Honest reflection.

And honest joy.

Living Out Loud

Over the years, I have decided to allow myself to experience joy. It was a conscious decision. And because I finally learned that joy doesn't have to ask for permission, and that it's normal to be happy, I am living my best life at 69.

But the journey continues. I don't have all the answers, and I still have a zeal for knowledge and growth, even at this old age.

As I've said, I live my age out loud. I celebrate it. I'm proud of it. And because I live out loud, gray-headed and all, I'm visible.

But over time, I've learned that visibility is not the same as validation. Being seen is not about applause or approval. It's about presence. It's about choosing not to disappear just because the world expects you to quiet down.

As such, my gray hair doesn't whisper, blend in, or pretend. Gray hair announces out loud, I'm here. I've lived. I'm still here. And I'm not finished.

Aging *and my gray hair* have taught me discernment, clarity, and, most importantly, what peace is really all about.

If there is a legacy I hope to leave, it's not about how I looked or what I achieved. It's about how I lived, how I loved, and how I showed up, especially when no one was watching.

I hope this book reminds you that visibility is not vanity. That confidence is not arrogance. And that aging is not the end of the journey. It is a continuation of becoming.

A gray-fully lived life is one where you keep choosing yourself. Where you stay curious. Where you take risks– even small ones. Where you keep learning, loving, laughing, and becoming.

It's a life where you grow more comfortable in your own skin, more compassionate with yourself, and more generous with others. A life where grace replaces urgency and wisdom replaces fear. And most of all, it's a life lived with intention.

For yourself.

For others.

And for the woman you are still becoming. *Gray-fully* and all.

ABOUT THE AUTHOR

Janice Cosby Adams, APR, is an accomplished author, marketing, public relations, and communications professional, and speaker. For over 30 years, Janice has led healthcare teams focused on brand development.

Janice's leadership and mentorship endeavors have earned her numerous awards and honors, including the Notable Marketer Award (Crain's Detroit Business) and the Community Mentoring Award (Results Mentoring) for mentoring over 100 young women throughout her career.

Featured in national and local magazines, including *Essence*, *MORE*, and *HOUR Detroit,* her image as a beauty icon is international.

Janice lives in Southfield, Michigan, and Wellington, Florida, with her husband, Dean. She has two adult sons, Brandon and Zachary Cunningham, and three grandsons, Harper, Brandon, Jr., and Kobe. This is her first book.

www.ingramcontent.com/pod-product-compliance
Ingram Content Group UK Ltd.
Pitfield, Milton Keynes, MK11 3LW, UK
UKHW062256290726
14090UKWH00017B/718